"Those of us who serve Unitarian Universalist parishes have seen it happen too many times—our most spiritually vigorous parishioners leave to join another church, even as they affirm how helpful the Unitarian Universalist experience has been for them. In *The Devotional Heart*, Morgan returns us to our roots in Pietism, the religion of the heart. He writes as more than a scholar: his life and work are expressions of this faith."

—The Rev. Frank Rivas,
First UU Church, Columbus, Ohio

"The vitality of Unitarian Universalism requires an appreciation of both our Unitarian *and* Universalist heritages. These two traditions that form our identity need each other. Until recently, Universalism was relegated to the sidelines. But the times are changing. Read *The Devotional Heart* and be renewed."

—The Rev. Dr. Thomas A. Chulak,
UU Congregation at Shelter Rock,
Manhasset, New York

"The tension between the head and heart, reason and experience, the individual and community needs to be kept alive in Western versions of the Christian commitment. The author speaks to this need by drawing on the scholarship and experience he has developed through intensive study and as a UU minister."

—Dr. Helmut Lehmann, Schiern Professor
Emeritus of the History of Christianity, The
Lutheran Theological Seminary of Philadelphia

"John Morgan has made a significant contribution to the spiritual renewal of contemporary Unitarian Universalism. . . . This book deserves to be widely read and widely discussed."

—The Rev. Dr. Charles A. Howe,
Lecturer in UU History,
Wesley Theological Seminary, Washington, DC

"The call to infuse rational religion with spiritual practice resounds throughout Unitarian Universalist congregations. . . . John Morgan suggests ways we may revitalize our congregations through small group reflective practice."

—The Rev. Dr. Lucy Hitchcock
Unitarian Universalist Community Church,
Hillsboro, Oregon

The Devotional Heart

Pietism and the Renewal of American Unitarian Universalism

John C. Morgan

Skinner House Books
Boston

Published by Skinner House Books, an imprint of the Unitarian Universalist Association, 25 Beacon Street, Boston, MA 02108-2800.

Note: The Unitarian Universalist Association is committed to using gender-inclusive language in all of its publications. In this edition, all introductory matter and connecting commentary have been revised to conform to gender-inclusive language. In the interest of historical authenticity, the documents quoted are printed in their original form.

Printed in Canada.

ISBN 1-55896-333-2

10 9 8 7 6 5 4 3 2 1
99 98 97 96 95

LET US NOT LOVE IN WORD OR SPEECH
BUT IN DEED AND IN TRUTH.
1 JOHN 3:18

To my friends and colleagues who have written comments about this book, I owe a continuing debt of gratitude: John Buehrens, who suggested the title from Hosea Ballou's works; Lucy Hitchcock and Tom Chulak, longtime friends and evangelists for our faith; Helmut Lehmann, a church historian and Lutheran who was my critic and helper along the way; Charles Howe, whose book, *The Larger Faith,* has inspired me; Fred Stefon, a friend and historian and first chair of one of our new congregations in Wilkes Barre, Pennsylvania (surely a place where we needed heart to start a church!); Frank Rivas, a spiritual mentor and friend who has taught me about faithfulness and courage; and thanks, too, to Brenda Wong, project editor, for her careful eye and thoughtful heart.

And to my wife, Cynthia, who has always been a person of the heart, and who, by her actions, has taught me more about what the Pietists meant by love than I shall ever discover in a book. I am grateful for this company of strangers, bound together in a community of spirit, a free church. They have taught me devotions of the heart.

CONTENTS

Introduction

The issue facing Unitarian Universalists entering a new century is that we often lack spiritual focus and depth, at a time when increasing numbers of newcomers to our congregations are demanding both. The decades of "Enlightenment" Unitarianism are ending. We can no longer see ourselves as an "alternative *to* religion," but rather as a powerful religious alternative, one that speaks not only to the intellect but also to the heart and the spirit. We also must learn to see ourselves as a community, a people—and not simply as individuals who happen to gather on Sundays.

Pietism is a way of life that can be found in many spiritual traditions, a religion of the heart that most church historians believe arose in the Protestantism of Europe during the last decades of the seventeenth century, especially visible in the classic text of this movement, *Pious Desire*, published in 1675 by the Lutheran pastor Phillip Jacob Spener. As a spiritual tradition, Pietism has focused on living one's faith as much as believing it (orthopraxy as contrasted with orthodoxy), the inward life as much as the outer, a return to the principles of community revealed in the early Christian congregations, the spiritual revival of personal and corporate life, and the application of the teachings of Jesus to social problems.

Though the term "Pietist" may have had a negative connotation (someone who is self-righteous and smug or wants to escape the world), the fact is that Pietism was for too long defined by its opponents; today, a wider and richer understanding of Pietism is being discovered in many religious circles. The title of this book, *The Devotional Heart,* illustrates how much Pietism influenced the earliest Universalists. It is taken from a quote by the great Universalist theologian Hosea Ballou, who wrote that Pietism means living the life of reverence, of devotion, in the depths:

> We must not look for religion in creeds or formularies of human invention. We must look for it in the honest, the pious, the devotional heart; in the heart which truly loves God, loves its [sister and] brother also. The principle of love to God and goodwill to all is true religion.

The remedy for our future is contained in our past. During a history course taught by Dr. Helmut Lehmann at the Lutheran Theological Seminary, I began to explore the Pietistic Universalist roots of our tradition, especially as they arose in Pennsylvania—specifically under the leadership of Dr. George de Benneville, a "radical Pietist," mystic, teacher, doctor, and student of native American religion and medicine.

In de Benneville's life and teachings, I encountered another model of a religious community—the "house church"—a gathering of many religious groups for worship, silent prayer, and action. The more I studied this model, the more I saw it as an early example of small cell theory in action. De Benneville's house church had all the characteristics of the model I was exploring: a small cell, people gathered in silence and prayers and readings from the Bible, shared leadership (de Benneville was not an ordained minister), common rituals such as baptism and communion, and a response to the community (often Native Americans might sit in the services). Our Pietist roots, strengthened by a new awareness of the need for public theology and institutional nurture, are the vehicle for our renewal.

The mission of our movement as it enters the twenty-first century is to revitalize its Universalist heritage, especially the Pietist part of the heritage (and most of the earliest Universalist leaders were strongly influenced by Pietism). But as a corrective to the separatist Pietism that neglected to organize itself institutionally, we can learn from the more churchly form of Pietism, which began with the work of Phillip Jacob Spener and his program for the reform of the Lutheran Church.

Spener's model for reform made great sense for our tradition. Spener called for the reform of the church from "right doctrine" to "right living" (orthopraxy), from believing to having a living knowledge of the Christian faith. To carry out his reform, Spener advocated establishing many small study cells or groups within the larger congregation, emphasizing the ministry of the laity, practicing toleration of different points of view, and focusing on the application of Christian teachings to everyday life. In Spener, I found the pattern of the early Universalist house churches—and a pattern that fits the contemporary needs of Unitarian Universalists.

Few books have been written on the Pietist heritage in Unitarian Universalism. The classic texts of Universalist history, including the definitive history of Universalism—Russell Miller's *The Larger Hope*—make little mention of Pietism. In Miller's defense, he states his purpose as to describe the denominational development of Universalism; since many of the early Pietistic Universalists were not interested in forming separate denominations, they are not included in detail. Clinton Lee Scott's *The Universalist Church of America* includes a chapter on the rise of Universalism in Pennsylvania, but it is incomplete.

The most complete account of Pietistic Universalism is an unpublished master's thesis by Charlotte Irwin at Tufts University in Medford, MA. Almost all of the major work on Pietism has been done by other religious traditions, especially the Brethren, Moravians, Schwenkfelders, Lutherans, and Methodists. I shall discuss many reasons why Unitarian Universalists have not, until recently, examined the Pietist tradition. By focusing our energies on New England we have missed Pennsylvania. Even when we encountered our evangelical ancestors, we might have been embarrassed. After all, in a movement dominated by the cool spirit of the Enlightenment, what could one do with a horde of evangelical circuit riders, Trinitarians, preachers who spoke from the heart, and people who lived far from Boston in the hills of New England or the rambunctious environs of Philadelphia?

"Roots and wings" are the words that best describe what follows in this book's discussions. "Roots" refers to the roots of Pietism. I will describe briefly the Pietist roots in Europe, paying special attention to the "parent" of Pietism, Phillip Jacob Spener, then to the beginnings of Pietism in America, focusing on the early Universalist Dr. George de Benneville. I shall summarize the forgotten Pietist heritage in Universalism and describe its fall from grace in the movement, by first looking at the evolution of Universalist covenants from 1790 and then briefly at Universalism's response to world religions. In each case it is possible to see how Pietism gave way to secularism, humanism, and the Enlightenment.

"Wings" refers to the future of any religious tradition. Here I look at the growth and decline of Unitarian Universalism and suggest the rise of a "new" spiritual hunger, one that bears a striking resemblance to our Pietist heritage. Finally, I will lay out a series of reforms that I believe are necessary to universalize Unitarian Universalism.

This book is intended as a broad, generalist essay and not as a specific description of one person or period of history. I hope to convey the dynamic of Unitarian Universalism, the movement from the past into the future. Second, not only has little been written by Unitarian Universalists about Pietism, but no one has discussed how to reform the movement along Pietist lines. I do not know if my proposed reforms will work until they have been tried. I have experimented with the Pietist small-group model and found it rewarding, but none of the reforms have been attempted systematically. I hope that what I suggest will be tried in a few congregations and perhaps discussed at denominational gatherings.

The primary audience for this book are those Unitarian Universalists who yearn for a deeper spirituality and are helping to make our religious community more powerful. To these people I hope this central message is clear: You need look no further than our Universalist heritage, especially the early Pietist strains, for strength and guidance. But I also hope that we have learned something about one of the major weaknesses of our tradition: its focus on inwardness and mistrust of institutions. This focus may have served individuals well, but it does little to create communities of people to carry on our religious tradition.

The spiritual renewal of Unitarian Universalism is a matter of ultimate concern. It matters to me whether there are people who call themselves Unitarian Universalists, not just for themselves but for the sake of the world. With all its weaknesses, Unitarian Universalism can model what it means to be a pluralistic spiritual community in a world sadly full of religious hate and deaths. That mission alone should be enough.

I hope that the renewal of Universalism will make us whole as a religious people, enriching our spiritual life and reconnecting us with religious traditions that share some of our Pietist heritage: The Society of Friends, Moravians, Methodists, Lutherans, Schwenkfelders, Brethren, and others. But I also am aware that the recovery of our Pietist heritage brings with it a judgment about our failure as a religious community to keep alive a significant part of our heritage and, in the name of a rational orthodoxy, to deny our own spiritual resources. No people can live in denial without suffering the loss of some dimension of their existence. Our loss has been spiritual depth. Yet it is not too late to recover our spirituality and, since it comes from the genius of religious liberalism, to restate it for a new century.

While I deeply treasure those Pietist Universalists who were separatists and yearned to cleanse the temple and restore a Christian community to the New Testament model, my reforms are based on the seventeenth-century Lutheran pastor, Phillip Jacob Spener. His reading of the church in his time, the facts of his life, and the reforms he proposed more than three hundred years ago are impressive. While I share with him some theology, such as his belief that all human beings share in a "common creation" and "divine love," I also acknowledge that he was a Lutheran speaking to other Lutherans.

Critics of Pietism have argued that by focusing so much on inner life and spirituality, the public dimension of one's faith is let go—people retreat into their own spirituality. To be whole, Pietism needs to feel deeply, but also to act boldly in the world. The second criticism of Pietism was that people could feel safe in small groups and remain there, removed from the larger body of the church. This, I believe, was the major problem with our fellowship movement in the past—they became havens, extended families, comfortable environments for like-minded people—and many fellowships died out. To be whole, small groups need to be connected to the congregation, not seen as something apart from it. While Spener's spirit and reforms fit the present moment in our tradition, his theology might not.

Pietist Roots in Europe and America

Because of its relatively obscure place in Unitarian Universalist history, Pietism, the religion of the heart, is seldom understood in its historical context. Within the last few decades, however, in many religious traditions (e.g., Brethren, Lutheran), interest in Pietism has revived, as well as a new willingness to understand its theological, historical, and ethical contributions to contemporary religious life. Unitarian Universalists have seldom been involved in this reassessment, even though Pietism was a major influence on most of the early founders of Universalism, such as John Murray, Hosea Ballou, George de Benneville, and Elhanan Winchester. There have been strong Pietist elements among Unitarians as well, not only the Transcendentalists such as Emerson, but also the founder of American Unitarianism, William Ellery Channing, whose focus on experience and character and a living faith relate to classic Pietist concerns.

It is necessary, therefore, to provide a brief overview of Pietism's development. A grasp of Pietism's roots is especially important for Unitarian Universalists, many of whom have no knowledge of its history or connections to their faith.

If we view Pietism as a tree, its roots would be the early Christian church. (For charts on the Pietist, see Appendices.) Many Pietists, of whatever time, have had the sense that the church of their time has been corrupted, and the necessary reform required a return to the pattern of the early Christian community. So Pietists might argue that Pietism begins in the New Testament.

One could also argue, as has Unitarian Universalist church historian George Huntston Williams, that Pietism's roots begin in the sixteenth century among such groups as the Anabaptists. Examples of such early "proto Pietists" might be Casper Schwenkfeld (1490-1562), Jacob Boehme (1575-1624), and Johann Arndt (1555-1621).

The European beginning of Pietism as a distinct historical entity can be dated to the 1675 publication of Phillip Jacob Spener's *Pia Desideria.* From Spener, two sometimes distinct but often interrelated Pietistic streams emerge: Churchly Pietism, and Separatist or Radical Pietism. While both shared common concerns—the feeling that the church had strayed from the New Testament, a call to holy living, the sense of God's presence, and the need for reform—they differed greatly in how reform might be accomplished.

Churchly Pietism's reforms were directed toward the reform of, and not separation from, the church; the goal was to continue and renew Luther's Reformation. Among the leaders after Spener was August Hermann Franke (1663-1727), who put into practice many of Spener's reforms. The center of such activity was the University of Halle, Germany, which sent some of the earliest missionaries to America. The major thrust of Separatist or Radical Pietism was to separate from the established churches to form communities more in line with what was considered the New Testament pattern. Gottfried Arnold (1666–1714) was an early leader; in the American colonies, especially Pennsylvania, Separatism influenced many Pietists, including some Universalists.

In terms of personal spiritual development and social impact, the Separatist tradition offers much. The life of George de Benneville shows that his faith bore fruits in the life of the wider community. But de Benneville did not start a church called Universalist; he organized no denomination. Believing in the unity of religion, he did not wish to splinter Christendom into greater divisions. For contemporary Unitarian Universalists, de Benneville provides an excellent example of a role model for personal spiritual growth and wider witness. He is a spiritual hero too long neglected.

For institutional spiritual renewal, Separatism is less helpful to present-day Unitarian Universalists. It provides insights into personal and social witness, but not into the renewal of whole communities. Indeed, excessive introspection coupled with attaching importance to religious experience provides the framework for an individualism that has made the experience of community so difficult. Rather, Churchly Pietism provides a corrective to the Separatist emphasis on personal renewal and a model for future community renewal.

The impact of European Pietism in early America was deep, diverse, and pervasive. From the Churchly Pietist stream came Henry Melchoir Muhlenberg (1711–1787), the early leader of the Lutherans. From the Separatist Pietists came many early leaders: Count Zinzendorf (1700–1760), Moravian; Johann Conrad Beissel (1690–1768), of the Ephrata Cloisters; Johann Kelpius (1673–1708), from a Philadelphia religious community; Ernst Christian Hochman von Hohenua (1670–1721), of the Brethren. Other groups, such as the Society of Friends, Methodists, Shakers, Dunkards, and Baptists were influenced by Pietism.

Pietist roots are deep in the American spiritual tradition, including the earliest expressions of Universalism in New England and the mid-Atlantic states. Pietism had great influence on most of the preachers and leaders of the earliest expressions of Universalism. Dr. George de Benneville (1703–1793), one of the earliest proponents of Universalism in America, is a main link between European Separatist Pietism and American

Universalism. Many early Pietists gathered to worship in de Benneville's Oley, Pennsylvania, house church. All of the early major founders of Universalism were influenced by Pietism: John Murray with Methodist Pietism in England; Elhanan Winchester, who was raised in the Baptist tradition; and Hosea Ballou, Universalism's greatest theologian, who was raised a Baptist.

The colony of Pennsylvania was a hotbed of religious fervor and Pietism. A haven for those who fled religious persecution in Europe, Pennsylvania welcomed many sects, especially German Pietists. New Jersey, too, was settled by people with Pietist leanings. At what is now Barnegat Light, New Jersey, in 1770 John Murray preached the "first Universalist sermon in America," though Pietists from the Ephrata Cloister had probably preached Universalism earlier there. Murray preached his sermon in a small chapel built in 1760 by Thomas Potter, himself probably a Pietistic Universalist, to await a Universalist preacher.

Though the Pietistic influence was strong in the mid-Atlantic states, it also influenced Universalists in New England. The first Universalist society in New England came under some Pietist influence simply because its pastor was John Murray. But elsewhere in New England—in the "hill country" of New Hampshire, Vermont, Maine, and western Massachusetts—a lively Pietistic Universalism flourished. Caleb Rich, Isaac Davis, and Adams Streeter became leaders of a radical, revivalistic, Evangelical Universalism that spread rapidly in the rural areas and small towns—a development quite different from the more genteel evolution of New England Unitarianism.

The rich and diverse spiritual heritage called Pietism raises the question: Why has it been so neglected by Unitarian Universalists? A few reasons are that our German roots and expression have received less attention than our English roots and expression of Pietism. For example, we know more about John Murray and the rise of Universalism in New England than about George de Benneville and the rise of German Pietists in the Pennsylvania colony. In addition, Unitarian Universalist historians have focused on New England rather than on the mid-Atlantic states. In general, few Unitarian Universalist historians are familiar with Pietism. Furthermore, some early Pietistic Universalists were simply not interested in forming a separate church called Universalist; hence they have been neglected (de Benneville's notes and some of his journals, for example, are kept by the Schwenkfelders, not the Unitarian Universalists).

Finally, history is written by the victor. With the emergence of a Unitarianized version of Universalism in the twentieth century (a more rational, humanized ethos), Pietism suffered from either benign neglect or outright hostility, because it represented to some a relic from the past. What some view as a relic from the past, others see as a treasure. Therein is the final irony: what some have rejected may become the cornerstone of the renewal of Unitarian Universalism as it enters a new century.

The Origins of European Pietism in Spener's *Pia Desideria*

If the Pietists were to have decided where their movement began, most would probably have pointed to the early Christian community, for here can be found the model for church reform. Others, particularly church historian George Huntston Williams, have suggested that a sixteenth-century movement that he calls "proto Pietism" arose as a third way between the Protestant Reformation and the Catholic Counter-Reformation between 1525 and 1575. In *The Radical Reformation,* Williams numbers among these radical reformers the Anabaptists, the Spiritualists, and the Evangelical Rationalists. He believes there is a link between them and Spener (Williams 1962, pp. 813–814).

Most scholars, however, trace the beginnings of European Pietism to Phillip Jacob Spener and the last two decades of the seventeenth century. Because Spener can be seen as an advocate for Churchly Pietism and because his reforms speak to the condition of Unitarian Universalism, I will discuss in detail the small book considered to be the precipitating force behind Pietism.

Historically, some thirty years before the publication of Spener's *Pia Desideria,* the Thirty Years' War had ended. Germany had been divided into two hundred territories or states, each governed by a ruler, whose power also extended to the church. The devastation caused by the war and what he perceived as the sorry state of church affairs, led Spener to remark in a 1669 sermon included in *Pia Desideria*: "How much good it would do if some friends would come together on a Sunday . . . would take up a book and read from it for the edification of all or would review something from sermons that he had heard! If they would speak with one another about the divine mysteries, and the one who received the most from God would try to instruct his weaker brethren!" (Spener 1675, p. 13).

In 1674 a Frankfurt publisher asked Spener to write the introduction to a new edition of Johann Arndt's sermons. Spener wanted to share his concerns about the plight of the church, but did not consider himself a reformer, as he reflected in 1681: "I could not permit myself the folly of appearing a reformer of the church; I realize my own weakness and that I have not the wisdom nor the power. . . ."

Spener's goals in the introduction were to "set down . . . most of the things that had again and again sorely distressed me. . . . I was aware meanwhile that countless others joined me in my laments. . . . The . . . spiritual body of Christ is now afflicted with distress and sickness. . . ." In the past, said Spener, church councils might have dealt with the sickness, but "if we wait for this to happen . . . we shall die before our wish is realized. . . ." Spener shared his thoughts humbly: "Let us remember that in the last judgment we shall not be asked how learned we were. . . . Instead we shall be asked how faithfully . . . we sought to further the kingdom of God. . . ."

Spener outlined the defects in his age among rulers, people, and clergy. Few rulers, he said, practice Christianity. Among the people, few practice the Christian command of love. He reserved his harshest criticism for the clergy, however, many of whom seem more intent on getting promoted than living the faith. Absent from many clergy, he believed, is the practice of piety; instead they judge "who is good and who are evil, not according to their life, but according to their doctrinal agreement or disagreement with us . . ."(Spener 1675, pp. 31-36).

Because of these poor conditions, Spener continued, those outside the church are offended by the differences between what the church professes and how it lives; those who love the church feel the same; and those who might join the church are turned away.

In the second section of *Pia Desideria*, Spener assessed the possibility for reform. He did not wish to create a "pure church" but one in which those who are not pure are not so conspicuous. His call is not to perfectionism, but to practicing, not just speaking, Christianity. Spener concluded the book with a platform of renewal. As do many later Pietists, Spener grounded his reforms in the Scriptures. He did not object to the centrality of preaching sermons, but that only a few portions of the Bible find their way into Sunday sermons. He hoped the Scriptures could be heard in their entirety by more of the people, and offered three strategies for doing so. First, every household should have a Bible and read it. Second, the books of the Bible should be introduced in Sunday worship, one after the other, without comment. Finally, the apostolic idea of small church meetings should be reintroduced, as outlined in I Corinthians 14:26-40.

The most far-reaching and important strategy was to establish small groups, or conventicles. Here lay persons and clergy could meet together under the leadership of a minister; they might read the Bible aloud, look for its meaning, and then "anyone who is not satisfied with his understanding . . . should be permitted to express his doubts and seek further explanation," a unique approach at this time (Spener 1675, p. 89). Spener noted that an added benefit of such groups would be that pastors would get to know their members more intimately, and vice versa.

A second suggested reform was to renew the spiritual priesthood of all believers, which Spener grounded in Luther's idea that "all spiritual functions are open to all Christians," (Spener 1675, p. 93). He argued that when spiritual functions are left solely to the clergy, the power of the laity is taken away. "The ministry," he noted, "is too weak without the help of the universal priesthood . . ." (Spener 1675, p. 94).

Believing love the mark of Christian discipleship, Spener suggested a third reform: Church members need to move from correct doctrine to right living (from orthodoxy to orthopraxy). He suggested that Christians enter into confidential relationships with others to see how they have practiced or failed to practice the commandments of love of God and neighbor. A fourth reform was the practice of love and toleration toward those outside the faith, "our brothers according to the right of common creation and the divine love that is extended to all. . . . Especially should we beware of invectives and personal insinuations . . ."(Spener 1675, p. 98).

The last two suggested reforms relate to the practice of ministry. In proposals that seem remarkably modern, Spener suggested that clergy be trained in the practice of ministry in small groups, with a mentor acting as teacher and friend, and in developing sermons that relate the text to the life experiences of the hearers (Spener 1675, p. 109).

Three major issues are critical to understanding Spener's *Pia Desideria*: his view of Scripture, because the

Bible was to him the source of church authority; his understanding of the priesthood of all believers; and the conventicles, because these were both the most opposed and probably the most powerful of his reforms.

Spener shared with his Lutheran friends the view that Scripture was central, but he differed in how he interpreted it. He believed that the Bible was meant to be experienced as a "living Word," not read literally, but directly appropriated into the lives of believers. He might have argued that no doctrinal interpretation of Scripture could substitute for a living knowledge. As Allen Deeter noted in *An Historical and Theological Introduction to Philip Jacob Spener's Pia Desideria,* Spener argued that the doctrine of the Trinity was not carefully outlined in Scripture and that a measure of personal interpretation should be left to believers (Deeter 1963, p. 183).

Spener's primary rationale for reform, however, was to renew Luther's call for a universal spiritual priesthood. All Christians may carry out ministerial functions, though laity are principally charged with ministry to their families and neighbors, while ordained clergy are the primary officers of church functions.

Finally, central to Spener's reforms are study classes in piety, or *collegia pietatis.* According to Theodore G. Tappert, who edited a version of *Pia Desideria* in 1967:

> If the church was to be renewed, Spener felt, a beginning would have to be made with the remnant of true Christians in every congregation. These had to be gathered and edified in private meetings in order that they might become a leaven to the whole living. . . . Contrary to Spener's intention, they sometimes became divisive. There was a tendency for the meetings to develop into little churches within the church (*ecclesioae in ecclesia*). . . .

According to Deeter, the small study groups probably began from a sermon Spener preached on the righteousness of the Pharisees (Matthew 5:20-26). Some hearers of that sermon were so enraged by Spener's indictment that they threatened not to return to church. But others were moved to ask how they might lead more righteous lives. He responded by inviting them to his home for instruction twice a week, a plan endorsed by his fellow pastors and the city council.

On Mondays, Spener repeated the main points of his Sunday sermon, with the group members seeking to apply the message to their lives. On Wednesdays, the group would read and discuss the Scriptures. At first, the meetings were attended mainly by persons from the lower economic classes, but later they were joined by a wide array of persons. Women were permitted to attend, but were seated separately from men. Over time, as the group grew and criticism mounted, the meetings were moved from Spener's home to the church.

Deeter says that a major problem for these groups was that they encouraged their participants to a radical Christianity that could not be fulfilled in the larger church. "The unsatisfied converts often became separatists . . . and would form the nuclei of separatist pietistic groups meeting and working quite independently of the larger body of the church" (Deeter 1963, p. 150). Spener tried to guard against this reaction by having ministers as leaders and moving the meetings to the church.

Pia Desideria was a profoundly popular work that engendered many reforms. It is not a particularly radical document in terms of style or theology. It captured what people were feeling about the church and offered alternatives. Deeter says Spener provided a "few exceedingly simple suggestions which were sufficiently concrete that anyone could put them into practice. Spener was not trying to teach the church anything new. He was simply lifting up again what many knew already but had failed to consider of great importance"(Deeter 1963, p. 208). Although later critics of Spener charged him with self-absorption or emotionalism, the lasting impact of this small volume remains impressive.

Separatist Pietism in America

Phillip Jacob Spener hoped to reform his church from within. But out of his movement arose Separatists or Radical Pietists who believed that instead it was necessary to form new religious communities.

One of the earliest and most influential of these radicals was Gottfried Arnold, who preached a mystical form of Christianity, contrasting those who had experienced a mystical union with Christ with those in the institutional church. If a believer had direct access to God, what need would there be for the meditation of church tradition or sacred text? It is at this point of "private interpretation" that later critics of Pietism insisted that it led to the dissolution of church authority and the notion of individualism. In *The Rise and Fall of American Lutheran Pietism*, for example, Paul Kuenning points out that Lutherans neglected Pietism for so long because they focused on its separatist branch, forgetting the classical form that was non-separatist, churchly, and reformist (Kuenning 1988, p. 3).

Though there are diverse and sometimes bewildering strains in Separatist Pietism (e.g., dreams, trances, near-death experiences), many Separatists shared four general themes according to F. Ernest Stoeffler's *Continental Pietism and Early American Christianity*: a deeply personal, transforming experience of God; house-churches established on the early New Testament church model; an aversion to theology and dogma and a faith in the power of the Spirit to lead people, related to their belief that they were ushering in the restitution of the true church; and a joyful anticipation of the Second Coming and the Restitution of All Things (apokatastasis), which is a major part of Universalist theology (Stoeffler 1976, pp. 164–165).

George de Benneville was not only a man remarkably ahead of his age, but a Pietist who had contact with European Pietists in Germany and Holland. His journal mentions his close relationship with Pietist Count de Marsey (1688–1752). Because so much of de Benneville's later life was rooted in Pennsylvania, it is important to highlight some of his religious environment, which one German writer, Albert D. Bell, identified in these terms: "In Pennsylvania, we have many religious opinions, but only one religion: the Pennsylvania religion of 'go a little, give a little, live and let live'"(Bell 1953, p. 31).

E. Digby Baltzell, in *Puritan Boston and Quaker Philadelphia,* describes Pennsylvania as an "ethnic and religious melting pot," fostering "egalitarian individualism," in contrast to Boston's more homogeneous community and "hierarchical communalism"(Baltzell 1979, p. 115). William Penn's policy of religious toleration helped to bring to the region an array of groups, many of whom had suffered persecution in Europe: Dutch and German Reformed, Dunkers, Moravians,

Schwenkfelders, Swedish and German Lutherans, Mennonites, Quakers, and others. By 1740, there were three major groups of immigrants: English, Germans, and Scotch-Irish. Although these groups intermingled, one Pennsylvania historian describes the early colony in these terms:

> The simplest way to describe the population of colonial Pennsylvania is to picture a stake driven into the ground at the waterfront of Philadelphia. A 25-mile radius from this peg would encompass the area of Pennsylvania settled mainly by English immigrants between 1680 and 1710. Extend the radius to the length of 75 miles, and the outer 50 miles of the circle would correspond roughly to the "Dutch" country from Northampton to York Counties. Here, from 1710 to 1750, the German-speaking immigrants to colonial Pennsylvania made their homes. Again, extend the radius to 150 miles, and in the outermost circumference, corresponding roughly to the arc of the Allegheny Mountains and valleys, the Scotch Irish settled from 1717 to the Revolutionary War (Baltzell 1979, p. 116).

Though the lines between various groups might be blurred, the picture is different from the more or less homogeneous confines of Massachusetts. Pennsylvania was a colony founded on the principle of religious toleration. Ben Franklin once asked Michael Wohlfahrt, a follower of Conrad Beissel, why his group did not publish their confession of faith. In words strikingly familiar to contemporary Unitarian Universalists, Wohlfahrt responded: "We are not sure that we have arrived at the end of this progression . . . and we fear that if we should once print our confession of faith, we should feel ourselves as if bound and confined to it, and perhaps be unwilling to receive further improvement. . . ." Franklin commented, "This modesty in a sect is perhaps a singular instance in the history of mankind, every other sect supposing itself in possession of all truth, and that those who differ are so far in the wrong" (Bell 1953, p. 31).

Yet Pennsylvania was also a battleground for winning converts, as new religious groups sought to establish their turf. No matter the religious tradition, clergy were in short supply. According to Stephen Longnecker's *The Christopher Sauers,* in 1740 there were only three German Reformed pastors for twenty-seven congregations (Longnecker 1981, p. 96). Most congregations depended on Europe for pastors, except for some of the Separatist Pietists, who started house churches without ordained clergy.

What set the early development of religious groups apart in Pennsylvania was that the free-wheeling sects seemed better equipped than some of the established

European church groups. Many of these sects came in groups; once here, they helped others come. Nor did they wait to have clergy to start their churches; many of their lay ministers supported themselves in other ways. Hence, as Longnecker notes, "A sectarian congregation could get rolling as soon as it organized and elected officers . . . "(Longnecker 1981, p. 98). A modern-day version of the sectarian congregations is the Unitarian Universalist fellowship movement, a network of free-wheeling, often anti-clerical, small groups started in the 1940s.

Clear connections existed between German Pietists and other sects in the Pennsylvania Colony. When William Penn and other Quakers gained control of West New Jersey in 1677, for example, they offered sanctuary to other Separatists from Germany and Holland. In 1726, 100 German Pietists emigrated from Wittenstein, Germany, to the Oley Valley of Pennsylvania, where de Benneville later was to settle. Longnecker cites that many of this group "hold the gospel of the Friends concerning the internal revelation of the Gospel. They hold, with the Dunkers, the doctrine of universal salvation" (Longnecker 1981, p. 76). It is little wonder, therefore, that when de Benneville arrived in the Oley Valley he was welcomed or that his journals are kept in the Schwenkfelder Library. The Separatist Pietists concentrated their settlements in the Oley Valley (now Berks County), and the Perkiomen Valley (now

Montgomery County), in land provided by the Society of Friends.

"For such a humble, pious, loving man I have scarcely ever seen in my pilgrimage through life," said the Rev. Elhanan Winchester of the first Universalist congregation in Philadelphia. Occasionally, Winchester accompanied George de Benneville on missionary tours. A summary of de Benneville's life, as told by Winchester, appears in *Some Remarkable Passages in the Life of Dr. George de Benneville:*

> Dr. de Benneville was born in London, England (July, 1703). He came of French Huguenot stock, and was the son of George de Benneville and Marie Granville, of Rouen, Normandy, France.
>
> In Dr. de Benneville's story of his life no reference is made to his scientific studies in Germany. Yet . . . he was zealously devoted to scientific study, including the branch of medicine.
>
> Following divine direction, he emigrated to America in 1741. The first person to greet him upon his arrival in the country of his adoption was Christopher Sauer, known in Germantown annuals as a printer and publisher. . . .
>
> Dr. de Benneville settled in Oley [Berks County], Pennsylvania, established himself as a physician, and began to preach the doctrine of Universal Restoration. Here he intermarried the

> Bertolette family. . . . About this time he built a large and substantial dwelling, in which a room was set apart for Christian worship; here, until his removal to Germantown, Pennsylvania, he lived and preached . . . the hopeful tenets of Universalism.
>
> Dr. de Benneville preached the gospel and practiced medicine, not only in Pennsylvania, in which he traveled extensively among the Indian tribes, but his active ministrations extended into Delaware, Maryland, and Virginia. About 1757, he removed to Germantown . . ."(Winchester 1890, pp. 45–49).

Although some of de Benneville's writings remain, by and large it was the influence of the man—not his works—that stood out, a factor that corresponds to the Pietist notion that a living Christianity is more important than a doctrinal one. Indeed, the transcription on a silver knife and fork presented to the family might serve as a motto for Dr. de Benneville's life: "Who trusts in God has built well. Who lives well, dies well" (Bell 1953, n.p.).

The deepest dimension of de Benneville's life was spiritual; he was, in Winchester's words, "in fullest sense, a prayerful man" (Winchester 1890, p. 57). His spirituality expressed itself in daily life: the study of the Bible; keeping notes of his life; family devotionals;

and preaching in his small Pietistic house church. He was, as were many Pietists, concerned with the inward person; he wrote in contemporary terms, "The Inner Spirit makes men feel that behind every appearance of diversity there is an interdependent unity of all things . . ."(Bell 1953, n.p.). He believed that every person carried two natures, an inner and an outer. The outer person is mortal, limited, concerned with the visible world. The inner person is spiritual, subject to sin, but capable of a relationship with God.

The theology beneath this spirituality was both Christian and Universalist. De Benneville wrote:

> Our faith is essentially the combined faith of all Christians and instead of increasing the divided churches, it is to bring them all into one, as truth alone grants. . . . Glorious truths are found in every church and nation under the sun. And this glorious chain of truth which some believe will someday unite all of them into one form of love (Bell 1953, p. 62).

De Benneville believed in and lived the theology of universal salvation. His words echo this theme:

> Preach the Universal and Everlasting Gospel of Boundless, Universal Love for the entire human race, without exception, and for each one in par-

> ticular. . . . Proclaim and publish to the people of the world a Universal Gospel that shall restore, in time, all the human species without exception. . . . He will restore all his creatures, without exception, to the praise of His glory. . . . My happiness will be incomplete while one creature remains miserable . . . (Bell 1953, n.p.).

De Benneville based his theology of universal theology on the Scriptures; indeed, it is reported that he helped Christopher Sauer produce the first German-language Bible, and in so doing, put the biblical passages that justified universal salvation in red type! Yet, as a Pietist, de Benneville believed that right living was just as important as right believing and his life mirrored this belief. He befriended the local Native American tribes and spoke to them of their "Great Spirit" as his own. His house church was truly ecumenical, inviting preachers of various persuasions to speak. And when he established a family burial plot in the Germantown section of Philadelphia he permitted British soldiers to be buried there during the Revolutionary War when no one else would allow it.

De Benneville believed it was his obligation to share the faith of universal salvation. Thus he journeyed not only throughout Germany, Holland, and France, but also to Pennsylvania, Maryland, Delaware, and Virginia. After settling in the Oley Valley he made frequent trips to Philadelphia and to the Ephrata Cloisters.

As with many Separatist preachers, de Benneville's chief occupation was not as minister, but as physician and sometimes teacher. He understood the interconnections between body and spirit. Six or seven of his remaining medical volumes contain notes on his practice that essentially deal with domestic medicine, "primitive medicine"—herbal remedies, some of which he learned from Native American healers. When he moved to Philadelphia around 1758 he opened an apothecary shop in connection with his practice and his sons were trained in medicine. His medical journals translate various native American herbal remedies into English or German to use with his patients.

Although Pietism is criticized for being excessively inward, to the neglect of the world, such cannot be said of de Benneville. His ministry to neighboring Native Americans is especially interesting. He said he had learned as much about botany from the Native Americans as he had taught them. He preached among them the "Great Spirit's" love for all humanity, declaring in language reminiscent of Joseph Campbell that "all symbols of the same truth are equally valid . . ." (Bell 1953, n.p.).

In dealing with Native Americans or other religious faiths, de Benneville tried to live out the requirements of his faith that the purpose of life was to work with the Creator in the salvation of all humanity and that while a single person remained outside that love, no one should rest easily. He did not have much regard for persons who defended the language of their faith without living it. "God judges men by their deeds," he wrote, "and not their creeds. The language of eternal love is expressed in actions. These speak more than words . . . " (Bell 1953, n.p.). The deeds of the orthodox, he felt, were often unchristian. "What wrangling, strife, schism, hate, envy, bitterness, murder and manslaughter, persecutions and wars! How much innocent blood was shed on account of factiousness among religions!" (Bell 1953, n.p.).

God is love. These three words might describe the heart of de Benneville's theology, faith, and the reason he believed that no person was beyond this God, whom he sometimes called "Our Sovereign Good" or "Infinite and Everlasting Love" (Bell 1953, n.p.). He wrote these remarkable words:

> The spirit of Love will be intensified to Godly proportions when reciprocal love exists between the entire human race and each of its individual members. That love must be based upon mutual respect for the differences in color, language, and worship, even as we appreciate and accept with gratitude the differences that tend to unite the male and female of all species. We do not find those differences to be obstacles to love (Bell 1953, n.p.).

In the following chapter we will look at the early Pietist themes of American Universalism and the covenants of Universalists from 1790 to 1984, which suggest that Pietism's influence on Universalism was minimal throughout most of the twentieth century.

The Fall of American Pietist Universalism

In the twentieth century, the oldest spiritual traditions of Universalism—Christian and Pietistic—declined steadily in influence as Unitarianism and Universalism moved toward an uneasy consolidation in 1961 as the Unitarian Universalist Association. The reasons for this decline are numerous and complex, but of particular interest are the following: as the movement became increasingly pluralistic, the Pietist roots were neglected; responding to the rise of secular humanism, the older Christian, Pietistic roots seemed out of place; and the consolidation of the two movements in 1961 was uneven—the much stronger Unitarian movement tended to dominate, while the Universalists were submerged. The result was the emergence of a sometimes theistic, sometimes humanist religion, with a stronger connection to the Enlightenment faith of reason than the Pietist faith of the heart. Finally, both Unitarians and Universalists had headquarters in Boston; hence, the mid-Atlantic expressions of the religion, particularly its Pietist roots, were forgotten.

Typology of Universalist Theology

Theological Type	Variant	Major Themes	Representatives	Special Features
CHRISTIAN UNIVERSALISM	Phase I: Redemptive Universalism	Redemptive *past*: the "good news" of God's action in history through Jesus. Christ's death has atoned for all human sin and made universal salvation a "fact."	**James Relly's** book, *Union* (1749) in England made the case for universal salvation. **John Murray**, the "father" of American Universalism (1741-1815), was influenced by Relly and John Wesley, and trained by English Calvinists.	Theology based on scriptural interpretations, not reason or experience. Was trinitarian, not Unitarian. Strong doctrine of sin. Earliest churches based in New England.
	Phase II: Unitarianizing Universalism	Redemptive *future:* Eventual restoration of all souls (creation), as seen in Origin.	**George Klein-Nikolia**, who wrote *Everlasting Gospel* (1743). **George de Benneville** (1703-1793), Pietist and physician in Pennsylvania. **Elhanan Winchester** (1751-1797), pastor of first Universalist church in Philadelphia.	Mystical, Pietistic, eschatological, evangelical. Started in Pennsylvania.

	Phase III: Jesus-Centered Universalism	No longer stress on afterlife, but on constancy of divine benevolence in all creation—and on human response to such benevolence.	**Hosea Ballou** (1771-1852), author of *Treatise on Atonement.*	Shift from the original roots. Ballou argued that the consequences of sin manifested themselves in this life only. Came to be known as "ultra-Universalism."
		Focus on ethics, "spiritual leadership" of Jesus, unity of God.	**Thomas Baldwin Thayer's** *Theology of Universalism* (1862).	Tended to be the prevailing form of Universalism in denominational life.
REPUBLICAN UNIVERSALISM		Similar to "American civil religion"—the view that Universalism represented the religious counterpart to democracy, and was the "religion of the future" because of its local congregational policies.	**Mary Livermore** (1820-1905), leader in suffrage movement; **Benjamin Rush** (1745-1813), applied Universalist principles to social ills (health, slavery).	Saw Universalism as the religious form of democratic principles and the "future church of America." Leaders often pioneers in anti-slavery and women's issues. Spirit of Enlightenment at work: values of free-dom, reason, etc.

Typology of Universalist Theology

Theological Type	Variant	Major Themes	Representatives	Special Features
RESTITUTIONIST WORLD RELIGION UNIVERSALISM	Phase 1. Universalism as "primitive form of Christianity"	Saw present church as corrupt and needed to restore church along lines of New Testament; found in Universalism what was believed to be closer approximation to early church.	**Adin Ballou** (1803-1890), founder of utopian community of Hopedale; practiced political nonresistance to war (Universalist version of "peace church").	Utopian, eschatological, critics of churches. Did not accept Hosea Ballou's position of there being no future punishment for sin.
	Phase 2. Universalism as emerging world religion	Saw Universalism as highest form of Christianity, but evolving into new world faith. Argued that Jesus taught a "natural religion," that Christianity was but one among many religions.	**Herman Bisbee** (1833-1879) argued against miracles, authority of Bible. Makes "humanity" the foundation of religion. **Kenneth Patton** (1911-) built church on this religion.	Devalued miracles and the Bible as sole authority. Tried to create a "religion for one world," taking insights from world faiths.

The gradual dissolution of American Pietist Universalism is evident in the flow of Universalist theology from 1870 on and in the evolution of Universalist covenants from 1790 to 1984 and Universalism's response to world religions. The typology of Universalist theology on pages 36 through 38 is based on George Huntston Williams's *American Universalism.* Though the theologies described here were prevalent in the Universalist church around 1870 and beyond, the basic categories still apply, although today there are slightly different emphases (i.e., the natural theology type would probably prevail, as contrasted to the dominant Christian Universalism evident in the past). To update the types, I consulted materials from Russell Miller's *The Larger Hope.*

Although the word Pietism is not identified in the typology, it is pervasive. All three variants of Christian Universalism are Pietist, although the unitarianizing of Universalism began with Hosea Ballou with a much greater stress on this life and the human response to grace. Phase I, Redemptive Universalism, is the most clearly Pietist, but Phase III, Jesus-Centered Universalism, might also show the practical results of Pietism in the life of the churches of that time, a Pietism that focused on moral living. Pietism is also found in the type called Restitutionist World Religion Universalism. Here, among such people as Adin Ballou, more Separatist Pietism again appears, with the prevailing themes of returning to the early Christian church model and separation from established churches. The beginnings of the separation of Universalism from its Pietist roots are evident in both Hosea Ballou's unitarianized Universalism and much more clearly in Universalism viewed as an emerging world religion, with a focus on natural religion and world faiths.

It is necessary to be clear about the central teachings of Pietistic Universalism, so we can later see what specific elements of the tradition were being neglected.

1. Creeds and formalisms are secondary to a living, tolerant faith.
2. God's love for all creation and the eventual restoration of all creation to "happiness and holiness."
3. A deeply felt need for a personal relationship with God, which could involve a conversion experience, possibly called a "theology of experience."
4. Reformation of the existing churches along New Testament lines, with an emphasis placed on individuals taking responsibility for their own spiritual developments, Bible study, and lay ministry.
5. While retaining the Bible as an authority, Pietists did not take it literally, but read it in the light of "the spirit." Experience was to be trusted much more than any literal interpretation.

6. An element of hope in the theology, leading to the search for the transformation of life in the present.
7. A focus on individual growth that may have supported the emerging critical reason of the Enlightenment.

Perhaps the most succinct definition of Pietism is given by Sydney A. Ahlstrom in *A Religious History of the American People:*

> [Pietism] was an effort to intensify Christian Piety and purity of life. At the outset it also involved a protest against intellectualism, churchly formalism, and ethical passivity. . . . Pietism was thus a movement of revival, aimed at making man's relation to God experientially and morally meaningful as well as socially relevant. It stressed feelings of the heart. It emphasized the royal priesthood and sought to revive the laity. It always called for a return to the Bible (Ahlstrom 1975, p. 236).

The Evolution of Universalist Covenants from Pietism to Pluralism

One of the enduring struggles for Unitarian Universalists has been how to create genuine bonds of community in the midst of a movement that places high value on freedom, especially on individual freedom of belief. The stress on human freedom is natural for a religious tradition with a more hopeful view of human nature than Calvinism offers and a fear of a centralized spiritual authority (because people had been burned at the stake in the name of orthodoxy).

When the movement was predominantly Christian, what bound Unitarians or Universalists together was a shared theological tradition as well as common stories and rituals. As the movement became more diverse, especially as it encountered and incorporated a new trinity of pluralism, humanism, and secularism, it became much more difficult to assert common ground.

While both Unitarians and Universalists throughout their histories have called themselves "creedless faiths" and provided "liberty clauses" in their statements of affirmation to protect the rights of the minority, in fact a master metaphor for helping to create community out of gatherings of individuals has existed. That metaphor is *covenant.*

Within the Unitarian tradition, covenants have been the means by which people have gathered together and called themselves a church for more than three hundred years. In *Walking Together: Polity and Participation in Unitarian Universalist Congregations,* C. Conrad Wright argues that covenants are the central organizing principle of Unitarianism. He traces this tradition to the 1648 Cambridge Platform, which defined the church in terms of a covenant (Wright 1986, pp. 7-8).

What binds Universalists into community has been less clear, yet from the first profession of faith in 1790, covenant theology has been the guiding principle: "We conceive a church to consist of a number of believers, united by a covenant. . . ."

Examining the evolution of Universalists since 1790 until the 1984–85 joint statement with the Unitarians, will establish three factors: 1) Covenants are contextual; they reflect the theology of the time; 2) Covenants change over time; 3) The evolution of Universalist covenants shows a movement away from Pietism and toward pluralism.

To understand the evolution, it is necessary to understand the word "covenant." It has both Jewish and Christian roots, but in contemporary language a covenant is the significant promises people make to each other and what they consider the ultimate in the context of their religious community. In *Mission Covenant,* William F. Schulz, former president of the Unitarian Universalist Association, wrote, "Covenants refer to the common insights and affirmations, derived from tradition and experience, that bind a religious community together in voluntary loyalty" (Morgan and Chulak 1987, p. 5). Also included in *Mission Covenant* is this definition:

Covenant is the central unifying promise or com-

> mitment that binds a religious community together in voluntary loyalty. It grows from an affirmation of shared needs, values, purposes, and principles. As such, it is rooted in the past, in the tradition of the congregation, and reflects the embodiment of the promise through history. It is a promise made in the present, with implications for the future (Morgan and Chulak 1987, p. 5).

During the summer of 1789 people with Universalist views, principally from Pennsylvania and New Jersey, met to discuss how to unify their movement. A circular letter was drafted and sent to all Universalists in America, calling for a meeting in Philadelphia. As Paul Chestnut relates in *The Universalist Movement in America,* in part, the letter said: "You no doubt have long since seen and deplored the unsettled situation we are in without order, rule and sistem [sic], floating about on the waters of unsteady and uncertain helps to promote or unite us in one General Church in bonds of love and uniformity" (Chestnut 1973, p. 59).

The letter found a response. Seventeen delegates attended the sessions from May 25 to June 8, 1790 in the Mason's Lodge in Philadelphia. The church in Boston appointed John Murray, who was the only New England delegate. Seven delegates were ministers, at least two of them Baptists. The only ministerial delegate from the Philadelphia area was David Evans, a farmer who doubled as a part-time minister. Other than Murray, the only other person from outside Pennsylvania and New Jersey came from Virginia. The Philadelphia meeting was the first time that Universalists sought to form a national organization, though they had gathered before. They adopted not only a profession of faith, but also a plan for church government.

The delegates to this meeting issued a statement, which is divided into four parts: a brief introduction, a chapter dealing with the articles of faith, a plan for church government, and recommendations for action (since authority was vested in local churches, this national gathering could not require action).

The central theological doctrine formulated in the introduction was that of God's love for all humanity. This doctrine was grounded in Scripture. The authors of this statement, one of whom may have been the physician Benjamin Rush, stated clearly what they profess in common in the Articles of Faith: "We believe the Scriptures of the Old and New Testament to contain a revelation of the perfections and will of God."

Based on this foundation, the authors argued the following: God's nature is love; Jesus is the mediator between God and humanity; the "holy ghost" reconciles sinners to God; and the purpose of the church is to promote a holy and useful life.

Their somewhat Trinitarian statement is grounded

in Scripture, acknowledging sin and the mediating role of Jesus, and identifying the purpose of the church in almost Pietistic terms as promoting holy living.

The statement also grounds authority in the local church ("congregational polity"), set no format for worship, had no official sacraments, described membership as simply subscription to the covenant, called for the establishment of church schools for members and the poor, and asked that an association of churches be formed.

The circular letter that accompanied the submission of this 1790 profession reiterated Universalism's central theological doctrine as God's love for all and the necessity of acting out this doctrine in love to one's neighbor. It called for a plan of church government that placed authority in the hands of local churches. This 1790 statement was by and large adopted by a later New England gathering and used to compose the 1803 Winchester Profession, which was much briefer, consisting of three paragraphs with an attached amendment. The Winchester Profession generally adopted the Philadelphia affirmations, again grounded in Scripture. The central theological doctrine of God's love was defined in Universalist terms as the restoration of the whole family of humanity to "holiness and happiness."

Although it followed the Philadelphia example, the Winchester Profession had subtle changes. References to Jesus as mediator and to the holy ghost were weakened. Theological skirmishes also may have given rise to the Winchester Profession. John Murray believed that all souls would be saved through a mystical union with Christ. Elhanan Winchester believed in the eventual restoration of all souls after a period of suffering. Hosea Ballou was wavering, wrestling with the notion that punishment for sin was confined to this life. Ballou already had challenged the doctrine of the Trinity. Here were the beginnings of the unitarianization of Universalism—the focus on this life and the human role in salvation.

Two other Universalist professions were drafted before the merger with the Unitarians in 1961: the "Chicago Declaration" in 1897 and the 1935 "Avowal of Faith." Before 1897, Universalists debated the merits of the Winchester Profession, some rigidly supporting its every word and others calling for reforms. In the Boston area, Universalist churches were surveyed to see what professions were being used. The only common denominators were the "fatherhood of God, the leadership of Jesus, and the ultimate salvation of all," according to Russell Miller's *The Larger Hope* (Miller 1979, p. 88).

This survey resulted in some amendments to the Winchester Profession, called the "Chicago Declaration," outlining five principles of the Universalist faith: (1) the universal fatherhood of God, (2) the spiritual authority of Jesus, (3) the trustworthiness of the Bible,

(4) the certainty of just retribution for sin, and (5) the final harmony of all souls with God. There was nothing new about the language, though some of the older Pietist phrases are missing (such as "happiness and holiness"). Miller called this statement a "truce of fatigue rather than the victory of any particular faction" (Miller 1979, p. 93).

The last Universalist profession before the merger with the Unitarians was in 1935, known simply as the "avowal of faith." This statement clearly was theist, although the old language of the trustworthiness of Scripture was gone, as were Pietist phrases. The core values were expressed simply:

> We avow our faith in God as eternal and all-conquering Love, in the spiritual leadership of Jesus, in the supreme worth of every human personality, in the authority of truth known or to be known, and in the power of men of good will and sacrificial spirit to overcome all evil and progressively establish the kingdom of God. . . .

To everyone's surprise, the statement was ratified unanimously in 1935. It was the last covenant of the Universalists as a separate religious body.

The covenant of the merged groups was no longer doctrinal. No mention was made of the scriptural basis of authority. Instead of a profession of faith or avowal, the bylaws of the Unitarian Universalist Association, adopted in 1959, substituted "principles of a free faith," naming six:

1. To strengthen one another in a free and disciplined search for truth as the foundation of our religious fellowship.
2. To cherish and spread the universal truths taught by the great prophets and teachers of humanity in every age and tradition, immemorially summarized in the Judeo-Christian heritage as love to God and love to man.
3. To affirm, defend, and promote the supreme worth of every human personality, the dignity of man, and the use of the democratic process in human relationships.
4. To implement our vision of one world by striving for a world community founded on ideals of brotherhood, justice, and peace.
5. To serve the needs of member churches and fellowships, to organize new churches and fellowships, and to extend and strengthen liberal religion.
6. To encourage cooperation with men of good will in every land.

Of these "principles" (the wording "principles" instead of "covenant" or "avowal" itself indicates the growing skepticism and secularization of the movement; "principles" is a much more neutral and less theological term), the second one—Judeo-Christian affirmation—caused the most debate. The principle, while acknowledging the Judeo-Christian heritage, places it as one among many other traditions of universal truth, preparing the way for religious pluralism. Without the second principle, one could subscribe to these principles from a plurality of religious orientations. And no statements bear any resemblance to the older Universalist covenants with Pietist leanings. In this first statement of Unitarians and Universalists, Pietism has given way to pluralism.

In 1977, the UUA General Assembly passed the Women and Religion Resolution; in the following years several districts and local congregations proposed revisions to the bylaws section of the UUA's principles. At the 1981 General Assembly a committee was named to draft changes; the result was a 1984 statement adopted by the General Assembly that still stands as the official covenant of the denomination.

The 1984 statement reads as follows:

> We, the member congregations of the Unitarian Universalist Association, covenant to affirm and promote:
>
> The inherent worth and dignity of every person.

Justice, equity, and compassion in human relations.

Acceptance of one another and encouragement to spiritual growth in our congregations.

A free and responsible search for truth and meaning.

The right of conscience and the use of the democratic process within our congregations and in society at large.

The goal of world community with peace, liberty, and justice for all.

Respect for the interdependent web of life, of which we are a part.

The living tradition we share draws from many sources:

Direct experience of that transcending mystery and wonder, affirmed in all cultures, which moves us to a renewal of the spirit and an openness to the forces that create and uphold life.

Words and deeds of prophetic women and men which challenge us to confront powers and structures of evil with justice, compassion, and the transforming power of love.

Wisdom from the world's religions which inspires us in our ethical and spiritual life.

Jewish and Christian teachings which call us to

respond to God's love by loving our neighbors as ourselves.

Humanist teachings which counsel us to heed the guidance of reason and the results of science, and warn us against idolatries of the mind and spirit.

Grateful for the religious pluralism which enriches and ennobles our faith, we are inspired to deepen our understanding and expand our vision. As free congregations we enter into this covenant, promising to one another our mutual trust and support.

Omitted from the statement of principles are most of the doctrinal issues from past covenants, such as the nature of God, the place of Jesus, and the destiny of humanity. Missing, too, are groundings of the statement in Scripture; instead, the authority appeals to multiple sources. The language itself—"grateful for the religious pluralism"—provides the clue to the master metaphor for Unitarian Universalism: pluralism. The task becomes how to create genuine spiritual community while affirming a plurality of religious views.

But while the emphasis of the new statement shows the impact of both Enlightenment faith ("Human teachings which counsel us to heed the guidance of reason"), some language that opens up Unitarian Universalists to an emerging spirituality is intriguing. Consider two of the values: acceptance of one another and encouragement to spiritual growth in our congregations, and respect for the interdependent web of life. Both these values are communal and relational, not ones that can be carried out in isolation. One of the sources of authority for these values—"direct experience of that transcending mystery and wonder . . ."—has Pietist overtones, if not outright mysticism. Just as the early Universalists stressed the realm of experience as the place where God speaks to human beings, so, too, this statement reaffirms it, speaking of "God" as "that transcending mystery and wonder"—the same principle.

Listening to people in our congregations—especially the newcomers—has taught me that of the principles in the UUA statement, two have become increasingly important: spiritual growth and respect for the interdependent web of life. Interest is growing in firsthand experience of what the statement refers to as "that transcending mystery and wonder." George de Benneville often spoke of the interwoven network of life, spiritual growth, and the experience of personal transformation; he may hold the keys to our future.

A review of Universalist covenants from 1790 to 1984–85 shows these evolving themes:

1. The source of authority has moved from a single source (usually the Bible) to multiple sources (human experience, reason, world

religions, etc.).

2. Later statements omit the old, decidedly Christian doctrines such as the role of Jesus, the Holy Ghost, or the classic Universalist doctrine of ultimate restoration.
3. The common values expressed have changed over time. Early Universalist covenants were grounded in the assertion of God's love for all creation—the master metaphor. Later covenants adopt more contemporary values, such as the free search for truth, a vision of one world, etc.

In short, the evolution has been from the Christian Pietistic roots of Universalism to a more generalized religiosity that is more pluralist, more humanistic, and often more individualistic. A 1981 denominational report on religious education, "Purposes and Principles: How We Got There" states this evolution well: "Our Association of autonomous churches and fellowships embraces a broad and diverse range of faith and value commitments, from Christian through Theist to Humanist. With common roots in 18th and 19th century liberal Protestant thought, all these positions are authentic Unitarian Universalist affirmations" (UUA 1981, p. 4).

Universalism's Response to World Religions

An early interest in other faiths led many Unitarians and Universalists to be interested in world religions, either because they contained "universal truths" or because it was felt other faiths illuminated the Christian faith. Both Unitarians and Universalists wrote about other world traditions and joined the World Parliament of Religions in 1893. Universalism's response to world religions shows a gradual movement away from its historic roots toward a more generalized religion.

In the typology of Universalist theology discussed earlier, Restitutionist World Religion was one variant in the movement and was represented by two branches: one that saw Universalism as a primitive form of Christianity and another that saw Universalism as an emerging world faith, apart from its Christian roots.

Universalism seen as a primitive form of Christianity shares concerns with the Separatist Pietists to return to the "pure Christianity" of the New Testament and to get away from creeds and orthodoxy. A primary figure here is Adin Ballou (1803–1890), founder of the pacifist Hopedale Community and author of *Primitive Christianity and Its Corruptions* (1870), which argued that not only Christians but most Universalists had strayed from the teachings of Jesus. Ballou established a new religious community in 1841 based on the New Testament and formally left the Universalist ministry. Ballou, however, remained true to the Christian roots of the Universalist faith, taking them so seriously that he tried to establish a religious community based on returning love for evil and living in unity. His community dissolved in 1859, another example of Separatists beginning but not continuing their communities.

Different in theological orientation from Ballou was the second representative of Restitutionist World Religion Universalism, the Rev. Herman Bisbee (1833–1879), who exemplified the triumph of the Enlightenment faith and was a harbinger of the more dominant variety of Unitarian Universalism in the second half of this century.

Bisbee denied miracles and supernatural proofs of divinity. He held the infallibility of the Bible to be a myth. Herman Bisbee's theology was heretical in its criticisms of the traditional sources of authority among Universalists. In short, Bisbee adopted a "natural religion." His words, quoted in Elmo Arnold Robinson's *American Universalism,* were clear:

> I believe that Jesus taught natural religion and claimed to teach nothing more. . . . There is no creed from his lips; no ceremony imposed. He would not persecute; he would not ask us to believe alike. . . . Salvation does not come by grace. All the priests in the world cannot pray a soul out of its natural purgatory. . . . Jesus taught good-

> ness, and this is Natural Religion (Robinson 1970, p. 31).

Bisbee's trial and eventual removal from fellowship in 1872 was probably the most radical step taken by the denomination to enforce its will, although the Winchester Profession contained a "liberty clause" that did not make it binding on any congregation. The denomination accused him of making human beings the ground of all religion. These themes represented by Bisbee later dominated the movement, moving it from a traditionally Christian base to a milder theistic humanism, undervaluing institutional life and focusing instead on social service and humanitarianism. Consider these words from Clinton Lee Scott's, *The Universalist Church in America:*

> It is observed that liberal religion has already moved away from many of the dogmas upon which the structure of Christianity rests. . . . The Bible is now understood . . . like the scriptures of other religions. . . . Jesus is not a supernatural being, but a man pre-eminent among the great prophets of the ages. Faith is not the uncritical acceptance of a creed but the free employment of the mind in the search for truth. Salvation is not the acceptance of Christ as Lord and Saviour, but the process of bringing persons to the full

> realization of their potential greatness. . . . The theological differences existing within the Universalist Church today are not mainly between reactionaries on the one hand and progressives on the other. They are rather between those who generally have moved beyond the Universalist position of recent generations. . . (Scott 1957, pp. 44-45).

Both Bisbee's "natural religion" and Scott's description above, offer a fairly accurate picture of where many Unitarians and Universalists have stood for most of the past half century. Universalists, like their Unitarian cousins, had moved from the Christianity of their beginnings to a more generalized religion of humanity. Yet after making the above statement, Scott made this intriguing, undeveloped assessment: "There is emerging a strong element of thought resembling the ideas which characterized the religion of de Benneville and his community" (Scott 1957, pp. 45-46). That religion is Pietism and it has emerged. A hunger for spirituality, for a heartfelt experience, has not disappeared. Rather, it has dramatically increased as the older Unitarian rationalistic orthodoxy has lessened its hold on the movement.

Pluralism and a rebellion against spirituality in the name of individualism were two dominant themes in much recent Unitarian Universalist theology and history, which may explain why a counterreaction is addressing two primary issues:

1. What binds, rather than separates, people into significant community.
2. How do we create genuine *spiritual community* with people who value individual freedom of belief so highly?

The next chapter illustrates how an emerging spirituality among Unitarian Universalists is developing and what it has to offer the future of the religion. Significantly, the contemporary spiritual expression has much in common with the older Universalist Pietism: a focus on religious experience, a protest against excessive rationalism, a search for a communal expression of faith, a desire for the social application of the faith in everyday life, and a religion of the heart based on the need for personal and societal transformation.

Growth, Decline, and Spiritual Ferment Among Unitarian Universalists

In 1983 the Unitarian Universalist Association's Extension Department asked me to look at the denomination's demographics of growth and decline since 1961, and to offer some general suggestions about my discoveries. I have used this research and updated it to 1992.

Membership declined from 1961 until well into the 1980s for factors both external and internal to the denomination. In particular, the unclear spiritual climate in which Unitarian Universalists traveled and their general resistance to traditional paths of spiritual expression were important factors. Many Unitarian Universalists defined themselves in opposition to other faiths, seeing themselves as an alternative to religion and not as a powerful religious alternative. As we have articulated our faith more clearly in the last decade, we have grown.

Many other demographic factors enter into the last decade of growth; but the struggle to reaffirm what we hold in common has been one major reason that newcomers have sought us out. In a pluralistic faith, a greater degree of particularity is required to avoid confusion; our 1984–85 Statement of Principles and Purposes was a major factor in our growth. From 1982 until 1992, Unitarian Universalism grew at the rate of about two percent (adults and children) each year. One of the reasons is demographic—especially the arrival of the baby boomers to our congregations—but another, less verifiable reason for our advance may be our new seriousness about what makes us a religious community, including the recovery of our heritage and identity and a new focus on communal expressions of our spirituality, such as worship and religious education.

There is also a great deal of spiritual ferment in the movement, especially about what constitutes "spirituality." My conclusions are based on both denominational studies and my experiences as a minister. I will argue that the movement is now experiencing the dying of an old mythology (the Enlightenment faith or Religion of Reason) and the emergence of a new mythology that bears the spirit of the early Pietists, if not their actual language.

Growth and Decline

Understanding church growth and decline is a risky venture, which does not often yield clear answers. As Dean R. Hoge and David A. Roozen indicate in *Under-*

standing Church Growth and Decline, four factors must be taken into account when considering such an issue:

1. National contextual factors: factors operating outside the church that influence growth or decline (such as the rise of the baby boomers).
2. National institutional factors: forces at the national level of the church (such as the merger of the Unitarians and Universalists).
3. Local contextual factors: the characteristics of a local community over which a congregation has little control (such as the relocation of a major industry).
4. Local institutional factors: factors internal to the local church (such as priorities and budgets) (Hoge and Roozen 1979, pp. 35-40).

What follows is a broad overview, beginning with a summary of the two denominations before the merger in 1961.

By the mid-nineteenth century, Universalism was a relatively large religious movement, often listed among the top ten denominations in the United States in terms of membership. From 1900 to 1950, however, the number of Universalist churches and their members dramatically declined. As Dorothy Spoerl notes in *A Brief Look at the History of Extension,* in Massachusetts alone during this fifty-year period, fifty-two Universalist churches closed while only two were added (Spoerl 1978, p. 5). Many reasons have been offered for this decline: a shortage of ministers, dying rural churches, the changing character of populations, and the failure of urban churches to respond to changing conditions. Two prominent reasons for the decline seem more relevant: the lack of organizational resources and the loss of a more controversial theology. Universalism thrived when it stood against the prevailing orthodoxy of Calvinism; as Universalism became less controversial, its sense of mission was dissipated. By the time of merger with the Unitarians in 1961, therefore, Universalism was at a weak point of organizational strength.

Conversely, from 1900 to 1950, a Unitarian renaissance occurred. From 1935 to 1957, for example, adult membership grew from 60,574 to 106,000. Enrollment in religious education for children increased by 169 percent. Surely the changing American culture of increased pluralism had an affect on the growth, but so did an increased emphasis on growth at the national level under the leadership of American Unitarian Association president Frederick May Eliot (1937–1958). In fact, the organizational qualities lacking in Universalism during the same time period—vision and organization—were the qualities Eliot encouraged.

The merger with the Universalists decreased the average size of Unitarian congregations, because many of the Universalist churches were smaller. While the merged denomination reached a peak in terms of both adult and children in 1968, from then on there was a steady decline. For example, between 1972 and 1982, the denomination lost almost 20,000 adults and the same number of children, a significant loss when the total Unitarian Universalist adult population in North America numbered fewer than 200,000. Also troubling was the loss of children—from a reported 105,000 in 1968 to roughly 36,000 in 1982.

During the same time period many "mainline" denominations underwent declines at least as troublesome as the one faced by Unitarian Universalists. But, as my 1983 report, "Growth and Decline Among the Unitarian Universalists," mentions:

1. We failed to understand the times in which we were living, especially the increasing numbers of people who dropped out of any religious tradition altogether. We did not lose people to more fundamentalist sects; we tended to lose people to no churches at all.
2. We failed to articulate a vision grounded in our heritage that might have spoken to the growing need for spiritual moorings in a culture of rapid change.
3. Many factors were outside our control, such as population shifts from New England to the South and the West (Morgan 1983, pp. 31-33).

One of the major vehicles for growth in this century—fellowship movement—needs to be singled out because this movement was in many ways a modern version of the Separatist Pietist themes, even though many of the fellowships believed themselves to be the grandchildren of the Enlightenment. Fellowships tended to be lay led, smaller, often anti-institutional in terms of traditional church organizations, with members of the fellowships carrying out most of the duties normally reserved for ministers. Though overtly rationalistic, these small groups shared much in common with the early Separatist Universalists: a focus on experience rather than doctrine, a protest against the established order, a search for a more satisfying sense of community, a focus on ethics, and a strong commitment to lay leadership. These fellowships were more humanist and individualistic, and differed from the old Pietist religious communities most strikingly in theological orientation.

Nonetheless, fellowships represented the major vehicle for reaching out to potential members. Peter S. Raible, in *Fellowships: A Report Card After Twenty Years,* estimates that by 1958 one-third of all new Unitarians (and the movement was Unitarian, not Universalist) had first passed through the doors of a fellowship, and forty-three percent of Unitarian churches were either fellowships or churches that had started as fellowships (Raible 1971, p. 2).

The Unitarian fellowship movement began in 1947 under the leadership of Frederick May Eliot and the lay leadership of Monroe Husbands. Their original goal was to establish a Unitarian presence in parts of the country where there was none—a network of free-wheeling, lay-led, independent liberal groups.

In discussions with Husbands before his death, I learned about the early organizing of these fellowships. According to Husbands, the idea for the fellowships came from a 1907 handbook, *Handbook for the Unitarian League of Lay Centers*, which had been discovered almost by chance. Husbands went around the country almost single-handedly organizing fellowships. His usual plan was to find a small group of interested people, correspond with them, and arrange a public meeting. From the meeting would come the beginnings of a fellowship. Husbands tried to stay in touch with the leaders, but could not keep up with the growth.

The strength of the fellowship movement was its ability to organize new groups quickly, relatively easily, and, like the early Pietists, without a ministerial presence. The movement was extremely successful in bringing in new people; it was less successful in keeping them. Raible's 1971 study of the fellowship movement reports that one-fourth of the fellowships had died; of those showing numerical growth, most had called ministers (Raible 1971, p. 4). As the first minister to two new fellowships, I know firsthand the strengths and weaknesses, the strong sense of lay leadership coupled with only a little growth in such fellowships.

If the fellowship movement represents an Enlightenment version of the Pietist house churches of the early Universalists, we can learn from its strengths and weaknesses. The empowerment of lay leadership and the recognition of different forms of ministry is extremely important to the vitality of a religious community. This insight is important for Unitarian Universalists today because the ministry has become more professionalized and specialized. We can also learn from the weaknesses of the fellowship movement, specifically its mistrust of professional leadership and organizational development—factors that might have helped these groups grow rather than die. Most importantly, a movement without clear spiritual roots cannot survive. By and large, in the beginning most fellowships saw themselves as alternatives to religion, not as religious alternatives. Such movements blaze for a time and then, without spiritual moorings, die.

Since 1982, however, the Unitarian Universalist movement, unlike most mainline traditions, has shown a slow rate of overall growth partly from the return of baby boomers to churches, for their children if not for themselves. But the twin strategies of vision and organization also seem to play a part. Unitarian Universalists, as the adoption of a denominational statement of purpose in 1984–85 evidences, have been struggling to be much clearer about what the covenant binding the denomination means; there is a renewed interest in articulating a theology and a doctrine of the church. In addition, at least in the 1980s, there was a refocused organizational emphasis on growth; a fully staffed Extension Department at the denomination's headquarters began to work on helping existing churches grow and starting new congregations.

There also has been a spiritual ferment in our midst, a sense of wanting more from our congregations than simply meeting our intellectual needs and a desire to reclaim the part of our heritage that speaks to our newest members. There is a correlation between our growth and renewed spiritual vigor.

Spiritual Ferment Among Unitarian Universalists

In *Blue Highways*, author William Least Heat Moon tells a marvelous story. He stumbles upon a Georgia monastery where he encounters a monk, about sixty years old, who talks about meeting Thomas Merton. During the conversation, the monk notes that he had been a Wall Street banker. The obvious question was asked why he became a monk. "Look—talking about the spiritual life is a lot of crap. You just live it!" he said.

There is a great deal of truth to the monk's response: Spirituality is a new buzzword, often noted as a need but seldom described and less frequently lived. Listening to some Unitarian Universalists, one has the feeling that spirituality is a cosmic tablet to be taken in regular doses to alleviate whatever ailment a religious community suffers. Of course, the ailment depends upon the physicians' point of view—for some, the illness is the lack of traditions, for others the exclusively masculine language, for others lack of any psychological support systems in the church.

No response to the issue of spirituality will satisfy everyone, but there are some responses to the question. Most simply, the spiritual has something to do with life—with life at its deepest, most satisfying level. In the Unitarian Universalist Ministers Association's *1992 Selected Essays,* one historian of our religion, David Robinson, defines spirituality among Unitarian Universalists as a

> feeling or hunger for a deeper inner life and a more profound experience of the world that we share. We're haunted by the specter of our own superficiality, the uneasy feeling that life is sliding by and leaving no deep mark on us, that we're being cheated of some version of real experience that would add marrow to the dry bones of our daily routine. We've found ways to dealing with this hunger, or masking it, but we've found it has a curious persistence (UUMA 1992, p. 24).

Although the third principle of the Unitarian Universalist Association is clear ("acceptance of one another and encouragement to spiritual growth in our congregations"), much confusion remains among us—sometimes perhaps deliberate, because we fear that in opening ourselves to spirituality we are opening ourselves to a power over which our reason may not have complete control.

As an experiment in 1991, I asked gatherings of Unitarian Universalists over a period of two months to openly discuss spirituality and what it means to them. I asked people to brainstorm, without argument, and simply list words they felt described spirituality. I came up with 120 definitions, but five were common to every group:

1. Connected to others, to Life, to God.
2. Wholeness, a sense of completeness.
3. Awareness of what is really important.
4. Centeredness, feeling at one with myself, with others.
5. Transcendence, something new breaking in, not necessarily self-induced.

Abundant life, a deeper life, a life of the spirit and not just the intellect, a sense of something missing in our religious life—all these get at the issue raised by Robinson: there is a hunger in our midst for a kind of life that our religious arrangements are not fulfilling.

Overall, Unitarian Universalists pride ourselves on being rational people, but our understanding of our spiritual ferment is inadequate. Few of the denominational studies have covered spiritual quality. Perhaps the best review of our spirituality was made by a study commission in the 1930s (*Unitarians Face A New Age*). Our movement needs a thorough, detailed study and analysis of the spiritual ferment among our own members, especially people new to our faith and those from the age group eighteen to thirty-five years old, because times have changed and we are entering a new century.

Generally, we also need to be clearer about what constitutes Unitarian Universalist spirituality. Ironically, we often turn everywhere else but our own heritage for guidance—to the East, to psychological remedies, to creation spirituality, to feminist theology—all of which are important, but without reference to our history, incomplete. Within our tradition, two forms of spirituality are uniquely part of our collective identity. One is Transcendentalism, the other is Pietism. Before leaving for India or therapy, we might consult our own religion for guidance.

Some Research About the Ferment

Little in our denominational life indicates that we have taken seriously the depth and extent of the current spiritual ferment. One of the purposes of the Unitarian Universalist Commission on Appraisal is to study and suggest approaches to issues that might be of concern to all Unitarian Universalists; yet, since 1968, only one study, *The Quality of Religious Life in Unitarian Universalist Congregations,* has dealt with the question of spiritual ferment—the rest have focused on structural issues (i.e., the study of districts, General Assembly) and only one has been oriented to social justice (a 1983 report on racial justice). Of all issues, spiritual identity is surely one that concerns a religious movement, yet our studies would not prove it.

The denomination needs to take a new reading on the emerging spirituality of its members, especially those who have joined since 1980. We might discover the spiritual needs and desires of our newcomers to be different from those of our longtime members. But at least as a beginning, we should respond to such fundamental questions as:

1. What are the spiritual needs and desires of those persons who have joined our movement since 1980?
2. Do any common spiritual concerns describe people in our congregations between the ages of eighteen and thirty-five?
3. How spiritually diverse are we as a religious movement?

4. How do we affirm diversity yet practice a common spiritual discipline that will bind us together into a significant religious community?
5. How do we help our children grow spiritually?

Although no single study deals with these questions, parts of three previous studies provide some insights into the spiritual ferment among Unitarian Universalists.

In 1973, Robert B. Tapp published a study of some 12,000 Unitarian Universalists, *Religion Among the Unitarian Universalists,* whose conclusion was to classify many in the denomination as "posttraditional," beyond traditional Christianity. Interestingly, the subtitle of Tapp's book, *Converts in the Stepfathers' House,* indicates an uneasy connection to the past.

Tapp found posttraditionality to be the major characteristic of the Unitarian Universalist movement. He found that people coming into the movement in the early 1970s were not taking over the faith of previous Unitarian Universalists—hence, their designation as stepchildren. Tapp writes:

> There is a clear sense in which the posttraditional UUs are religious dropouts in relation to the Jewish and Christian outlooks that dominated the Western Culture in its formative periods. Furthermore, it may be noted that dropping out is an

> active rather than passive process. They have identified themselves with a presumably new and different form of religion (Tapp 1973, p. 195).

The central element of the Unitarian Universalist religious experience, according to Tapp, was conversion, not to be confused with the more emotional conversion experience of some religious groups. Rather, it was a gradual conversion experience—away from the childhood religion to Unitarian Universalism. It has been estimated that from eighty to ninety percent of the movement today includes converts from other faiths.

In assessing personal beliefs and attitudes, Tapp discovered the following:

- twenty-eight percent felt that "God" was a harmful concept
- sixty-three percent seldom or never prayed
- seventy-three percent felt the most important part of a church service was "intellectual stimulation"
- only sixteen percent felt that Jesus' teachings were still valid
- forty-three percent defined their religion as Christian
- sixteen percent felt closest in beliefs to Ethical Culturists (Tapp 1973, pp. 223-250)

Tapp is probably right in describing the movement as "posttraditional," but his assessment needs to be placed within the context of the times: the Vietnam War, tremendous social and political crises, and changes in personal value systems, especially with regard to sexuality. Within such a framework, churches were not insulated. A decided anti-institutional thrust permeated American culture at the time. Much of the change described by Tapp follows that pattern. It is no coincidence that during this time the fellowship movement was growing.

A less far-reaching study of Unitarian Universalists was the 1979 Media Feasibility Study. Although the participants in this study still ranked "intellectual stimulation" as a primary importance in Sunday programs, "emphasizing the spiritual" and "focusing on the heritage of the movement" were listed as ways to improve the local church. Interestingly, of the new members surveyed, eighty-six percent found some understanding of the word "God" acceptable, though the definition also included God as a name for a natural process in history. In 1967, twenty-three percent of those surveyed found "God" to be the basis of all being, while in 1979 thirty-three percent agreed; in 1967, twenty-eight percent of those surveyed found the concept of "God" harmful; among newer members in 1979, this figure had dipped to fourteen percent (Morgan 1983, p. 25).

A 1989 survey of 1,286 Unitarian Universalists (*The*

Quality of Religious Life in Unitarian Universalist Congregations), provides the most detailed picture of the spiritual ferment among Unitarian Universalists, although it lacks a specific focus on the emerging spirituality of younger and more recent members and an in-depth discussion of how the denomination could respond to their spiritual needs.

In terms of the nature of worship, while intellectual stimulation still ranks high, there is a new interest in the communal dimension. The report noted: "There is a trend toward being more 'overtly religious,' that is, valuing aspects traditionally associated with religious worship. This is strongest among young adults, women, and other 'marginalized people'" (UUA 1989, p. 5).

The communal, spiritual parts of the worship were greatly valued, though not always present in our services. In addition to preaching skills, ministers' skills in spiritual leadership and dealings with people were highly valued.

The report notes ferment in the movement with regard to ideas about God. Seventy-seven percent of those surveyed found one of these statements about God closest to expressing their beliefs: (1) "God is the ground of being"; (2) "God may approximately be used as a name for some natural process within the universe, such as love." Again, contrast the differences between this and the 1967 surveys: In 1989, two percent of those surveyed felt the concept of God to be harmful; in 1967,

28 percent felt the same. Though the sample of African Americans was tiny, it is interesting that almost no one had difficulty with the word "God"; most prayed and twenty-eight percent identified themselves as Christian or Christian Humanist. In a denomination of few African Americans (less than one percent), perhaps the prevailing intellectual worship style and lack of spiritual language are among the main barriers.

Sixty-nine percent of those questioned in the 1989 survey felt Jesus' teachings were still useful and true for today's life. Sixty-eight percent rated "spiritual growth" as vital to the quality of their congregation, yet only nineteen percent ranked their congregation high in terms of meeting this need. Only thirteen percent never prayed; fifty-seven percent prayed often or occasionally. Almost fifty percent identified "the divine" as either a Creative Force or the Highest Potential.

Again, the 1989 report notes that the desire to make the movement into a more or less humanist organization has dissipated. "The survey results . . . show the old humanist-theist controversy is passé. Rather, responses indicate a . . . human-focused religiousness, rooted in a sense of relatedness to trans-human cosmic process or power, not 'supernatural' but continuous with humans and their universe" (UUA 1989, p. 31).

Only among a people struggling with rationality would such a statement appear! Among the Unitarian Universalists surveyed there is spiritual ferment about the most fundamental questions: What is the meaning of my life? What or who is God? What is worship? And what is spiritual about my religious community?

In the fall of 1991, I journeyed around our congregations asking people what spirituality meant to them, since it seemed to be a need, but a fuzzy one. In six different groups in six different areas, some common themes emerged, which I have categorized in order of importance: connectedness, centeredness, wholeness, awareness, and transcendence.

In every group, one theme emerged: connectedness. It was expressed in various ways: "community and connection," "connectedness of all life forms," "connections," "connected with the oneness of all Being," "connected to Creation," and "connected to God." One group of seventeen people brainstormed about this "connectedness":

Connectedness: To what or whom?

- to other beings who want to preserve the universe
- to inner voice
- transcendental connectedness
- to other people
- to God
- to all living beings
- to the source of our being and all Creation
- to the past and future

Connectedness: How and where?

- through other people
- in your heart
- by going in and going out
- reflection, prayer
- good works
- life
- anywhere, all times, in front of us
- in the spaces of Life we make.

There is a movement in spiritual communities between inwardness and outwardness, between mysticism and propheticism. In *An Examined Faith*, theologian and social ethicist Dr. James Luther Adams noted these as the "eschatological" and the "mystical" elements in religion—the concern for history and time and the transcendence of each. Adams would have us maintain both elements in tension—being mystics but also prophets (Adams 1991, p. 48).

Unitarian Universalists, during much of the period from 1960 to 1970, were prophets, often neglecting personal piety and burning out. The late 1980s and early 1990s have seen the opposite approach, a kind of retreat into piety. It is interesting that the 1989 survey revealed little in the way of public religion. A time of tension is upon us, when the private and public dimensions of our new spirituality may yield powerful new expressions of what it means to be a spiritual community. Unitarian Universalist spirituality, therefore, needs to take into account three dimensions of the religious life:

The Personal: taking care of our spiritual needs, being responsible for our own development through regular spiritual disciplines such as prayer, meditation, and silence.

The Interpersonal: taking care of ourselves in relationship to others, especially those with whom we interact on a regular basis.

The Intrapersonal: taking care of our world, the strangers in our midst, those with whom we do not have daily interaction, those who have difficulty caring for themselves.

Identity and Spirituality

The question of identity may be the central question of an emerging Unitarian Universalist spirituality. The question of identity here is not individualistic (my identity), but communal (our identity). The kinds of questions to address as part of the communal identity question are: What is our heritage? What binds us into a significant religious community now? What are metaphors, symbols, rituals that represent our deepest held values? And what must we do in the world to fulfill our mission?

The need to move from individualism to some form of communal identity was expressed by one of the members of the 1989 study commission: "The practical and perhaps theological dilemma for us is to find a way to live in community, bound together because we need one another, and yet to do this without submerging or betraying our individuality. The danger that we face is that in overly affirming the individual, we become . . . atomistic. . . ."(UUA 1989, p. 3). Herein is expressed the continuing paradox of Unitarian Universalism: how to create and sustain commitments to genuine community.

The question of identity can best be understood in light of congregational studies (as included in the *Handbook for Congregational Studies* by Jackson W. Carroll, Carl S. Dudley, and William McKinney). The authors describe a congregation in terms of four dynamics: program, process, context, and identity. The identity of a congregation (or a religious movement) is a "persistent set of beliefs, values, patterns, symbols, stories and style that makes a congregation unique" (Carroll, Dudley, and McKinney 1986, p. 21). The identity of a religious group distinguishes it from its environment; the group may change over time, but the dominant factors remain.

The *Handbook for Congregational Studies* describes

seven ways of looking at the issue of identity: history, heritage, world view, symbols, ritual, demography, and character. One suggestion I would make for Unitarian Universalism is to focus on the question of identity and to wrestle with and describe how these seven dynamics function within Unitarian Universalism. The denomination as a whole and its Commission on Appraisal in particular should engage in a study of sufficient depth and quality to respond to these questions of identity.

History as one dimension of a movement's identity is the act of remembering, of sharing significant happenings. One part of our history—the Universalist Pietist, especially in the mid- Atlantic states—has been obscured, if not lost. A renewal of this aspect of our own history might pave the way for a renewal of our spirituality. While our historians may not have been involved in the renewal of Pietistic scholarship, we might approach others—such as Lutherans, Moravians, Brethren, etc.—to remember.

Heritage refers not just to history, but to something more: a religious community's acknowledgment of the inheritance of beliefs that make it unique, the "sacred deposit from its total past" (Carroll, Dudley, and McKinney 1986, p. 25). A whole part of our heritage, the Pietist, has been submerged, barely acknowledged. In a real way, the reclaiming of this part of our heritage would be a highly significant step toward wholeness. Here it would be necessary for Unitarian Universalists to learn from other religious bodies about our own heritage and to gather affirmations, stories, writings, music, and liturgies from the past.

The world view of a religious community is similar to heritage, but it is more our perspective for making sense of our life. One of the areas in which a religious community is bound together is the roughly similar world view its members hold in common. Do Unitarian Universalists share any world view? Little data supports conclusions, but assumptions are being made all the time that assume we know otherwise about the kinds of worship, forms of religious education, and social justice projects that we all support. More than one minister has felt the wrath of a church member after expressing what he or she feels is a common Unitarian Universalist value (i.e., reproductive freedom of choice), only to discover a significant number of people don't feel the same way. A major denominational study of world view might tell us not only our world views, but also differences in world views among age groups in our movement.

Symbols are another way to assess identity. Unitarian Universalists tell each other that except for the flaming chalice (even this is questionable), we have no symbols. Of course, this view is simply not the case. All anyone need do is enter our buildings. Where is the pulpit? What pictures are on the walls? What's on the front table? How are the seats arranged? All these, and many more, are symbols. While Unitarian Universalists claim they have no symbols, woe be to the person who moves something from the front altar! A significant project would be to analyze the various symbols and their meanings from a sampling of our churches to create a picture of our communal identity.

Ritual is repetitive action through which a group communicates what is of ultimate significance to it. Unitarian Universalists last produced a hymnal in 1964. A new hymnal, the first really to capture the movement in its current expression, is now available. As one of the few common books used in most churches, the new hymnal is an important key to Unitarian Universalist spiritual identity. Indeed, a review of the new hymnal—its choices of hymns, readings, etc.—would be a way to analyze the emerging identity.

Demography is a way to describe the characteristics of a religious movement. The 1989 study on congregational life is a demographic study. However, more demographics are needed on the baby boomers who are joining our congregations. Who are these people? What are their spiritual needs and those of their children? Are they different from, or like, baby boomers joining other religions? Answers to these questions would provide some insights and resources for the future.

Character is the personality of a religious movement, its special niche that distinguishes it from other groups. This area builds less on hard data, and more on what social scientists call "process evaluation" or "participant observation." What is the personality of Unitarian Universalism? Our advertising campaigns are based on the assumption we have answered this question. One small step would be to gather a team to conduct such an assessment in a few major regions, asking questions about our character, much as focus groups do for political candidates.

Ultimacy and Intimacy

Until recently, the words "spiritual community" may have seemed oxymoronic when applied to Unitarian Universalists. Unitarian Universalists have focused on "individual freedom of belief" rather than congregational covenants and on "reason" rather than spirituality. These two factors—individualism and a fuzzy intellectualizing about theology—resulted in the decline of the movement into the early 1970s.

More recently, interest has resurged in what binds our people together into a religious community, along with a profound wrestling with theological issues. The reemergence of interest in creating and sustaining spiritual community is the power behind our movement's numerical and qualitative growth.

In *An Examined Faith,* Dr. James Luther Adams offers a description of the nature of religious community. When asked at a gathering about what "made him tick," he responded that the principle things that concerned him were ultimacy and intimacy. By "intimacy," he meant more than social fellowship, something far deeper, more in the nature of the human drive for fellowship—what Aristotle said of the human being as an "associating being." Dr. Adams would say that the quality of one's associations sets the tone for the meaning of one's existence. By "ultimacy," Adams means what some might call "Transcendence" or "God," but neither word is indispensable. In what or whom do you place your ultimate confidence? The notion of "ultimate concern" comes from the Protestant theologian Paul Tillich, a close friend and co-worker of Adams.

These two dynamics—ultimacy and intimacy—have been weakened among Unitarian Universalists until the 1980s. This weakening may account for some of the denomination's decline. The two reasons people say they come to church are to discover a place to belong (intimacy) and to find a place that can provide some meaning (ultimacy).

For Unitarian Universalists to grow in quantity and quality, what is required is an awakened sense of the ultimacy of the Transcendent and a deepened awareness of our interconnectedness to one another.

Believing in free association and a non-creedal church, Adams would agree with the theologian Friedrich Schleiermacher that the function of the church is to bring together people with a variety of religious experiences—and to "exchange" experiences (Adams 1991, p. 21). I have sought to employ this process in new Unitarian Universalist congregations.

Spiritual Renewal Among Unitarian Universalists: A Pietist Approach

If spirituality in its most general form has to do with a hunger for greater life and community, such a spiritual renewal is at work among Unitarian Universalists. This renewal can be seen from the limited studies that show an increased interest in the movement in worship, religious education for children, and a greater sense of continuity with the past; and it can be experienced by those who have been part of recent growth, with many newcomers arriving with a desire for greater spiritual depth.

Five fundamental spiritual themes of Pietism have meaning for an emerging Unitarian Universalist spirituality.

1. *The Pietists were more concerned with experiencing the Christian faith, with life, than with correct doctrine.* They considered themselves to be completing the Reformation by carrying its reforms from the domain of theologians to ordinary people. Theirs was a religion of the heart and spirit, grounded in a deeper understanding of the Bible. *Similarly, the growing spirituality of Unitarian Universalists seeks a religion of experience, as much of the heart*

and spirit as the head. Discussing the left wing of the Reformation, from which sprang many principles of Unitarian Universalism, Adams wrote in *On Being Human Religiously*: "And rather than finding their defense in the rational individual, they typically appealed to belief in the freedom of the spirit"(Adams 1976, p. 8). Ironically, the new spiritual emphasis on experience and the spirit is rooted in Unitarian Universalist history. What probably differs is that the emerging spirituality does not ground its religion in the Bible, but adopts a much more symbolic view of its contents than the early Pietists would have.

2. *The early Pietists were convinced of the need to extend the doctrine of the priesthood of all believers* in the face of what many perceived to be a corrupt clerical system. Phillip Jacob Spener, for example, created small study classes for such a purpose. So too, there is a perceived need for the "ministry of the laity" in contemporary Unitarian Universalism, even when the professionalization of the ministry seems to be the rule. In *On Being Human Religiously*, Adams wrote:

> The Left Wing of the Reformation, therefore, also insisted that the church is a lay church; it is not to be controlled by "officials". Every child of God has the guidance of conscience, for the Holy Spirit is available to every child of God. But this conscience and the living presence of the Holy Spirit

> is found in the mutuality of community (Adams 1976, p. 89).

Until there is as much emphasis on the renewal of lay ministry in Unitarian Universalism as there now is on ministerial renewal, spiritual rebirth will not be complete.

3. *Many of the Pietists, Universalists included, felt the conversion experience central to their faith.* Orthodoxy was not enough; a changed life was required. Hence, in spite of criticisms to the contrary, the Pietist faith did have social implications, which lead to the creation of orphanages, programs for poor people, and universities. *Although contemporary Unitarian Universalists use different language, the conversion experience is the single most common experience they share*—with some ninety percent of our members coming from other religious traditions. Contemporary conversion experiences differ from the Pietists' form of sometimes emotional, immediate change; among Unitarian Universalists the change is more gradual, less emotional, but nonetheless an evolving one. How it translates into a greater social consciousness is an area yet to be understood.

4. *The Pietists rebelled against the oppression of the spirit, whether promulgated by the state or the church, the arm of the state.* While modern Unitarian Universalists talk about "individual freedom of belief," the early Pietists believed freedom of belief was not so much individual as communal. German Pietists did not come to Pennsylvania

to find an individual's right to worship and believe. This spiritual understanding is still strong, though there seems to be a deeper appreciation among newer members of the need for communal and not just individual expressions, for spiritual discipline and not just intellectual freedom.

5. *The Pietists concerned themselves with the search for authentic community*, especially one more closely identified with the early Christian community of the New Testament. Some radical Pietists felt the need to separate from the world to find such a community, while others sought to reform existing institutions. *Among many Unitarian Universalists today, the need for authentic community is perhaps one of the strongest spiritual needs*—maybe the result of preaching the doctrine of individualism for so long.

Given who we are, and where we are, what must we do? This question was the central one that I and Tom Chulak raised as the key to the future of Unitarian Universalism in *Mission Covenant.*

Who we are is a question of identity. We are more clear about our New England roots and the rationalistic version of our heritage than we are of our mid-Atlantic roots and evangelical heritage. Part of the recovery of our identity rests with our willingness to reclaim our Pietistic roots, which will help us be clearer about our spiritual heritage.

Where we are is a question of context. By and large, we are highly educated, mostly white, of higher income, and suburban. This is the current situation, but perhaps not the context for our future. To be whole, the movement needs to diversify—economically, racially, culturally, and geographically. One of the resources for creating the climate for such change is our Pietist roots, which go deep into city, small-town, and blue-collar cultures.

What we must do is a question of mission. We are witnessing the birth of a post-Enlightenment spirituality wider than Unitarian Universalism, but in which Unitarian Universalism can find a home. Our Pietist heritage offers us a spiritual tradition, a faith of the heart, a life of the spirit in community, the ecumenicity to enable us to reach out to others with whom we share a common past, and a chance to be whole. The myth of the Enlightenment, as James Luther Adams wrote in *The Prophethood of All Believers*, "lacked the sense of intimacy and mystery," while the Romantic reaction lacked the sense of history and community in the name of the individual (Adams 1986, p. 122). The emerging Unitarian Universalist spirituality needs to display both intimacy and ultimacy, a feeling for the presence of mystery and a willingness to take time—which is to say, history—seriously.

Universalizing Unitarian Universalism

Writing in 1941 in *The Christian Leader*, a Universalist publication, R. S. Kellerman responded to a friend's question: "Why the decline of Universalist churches?" The writer's friend lamented that in his part of the country, northeastern Pennsylvania, there had been seven Universalist churches. Only two remained. Kellerman offered seven reasons for the decline of Universalism:

1. Initially, the gospel of Universalism was strongly opposed; the more opposition, the larger the movement grew in response to the opposition, the more energy flowed. However, Universalists lacked organization; they did not consolidate the growing number of newcomers into churches.
2. The Universalists lacked discipline and effective government, hence, they could not arrest the decline. The authority that existed was invested in local churches. The Universalists resembled Presbyterians in terms of organiza-

tional structure, but acted like Congregationalists in terms of how they behaved.

3. Many Universalist affirmations (the goodness of God, the worth of individuals) were taken over by other denominations, therefore a separate Universalist denomination was not required.
4. Many small towns lacked ministers.
5. The Universalists had relied too much on the intellectual side of religion and too little on the emotional, sensual part of religion, often best expressed in worship.
6. Universalists had failed to respond to findings of science.
7. Society had become secularized, the work had changed, and the religious needs of many were no longer addressed by Universalism (*The Christian Leader*, February 1, 1941, pp. 107-108).

The reasons Kellerman cited for the decline of Universalism in 1941 might well apply to the weakened position of Universalism today. Universalism remains an unorganized part of the wider Unitarian Universalist movement. It still has no authority and its vision is weakened. Few focus on the renewal of Universalist heritage churches, especially in smaller towns and cities. And both secularism and humanism so dominated parts of the movement during the second half of this century that much of our older heritage was lost.

At the end of his article, Kellerman asked his friend, "What is the remedy? How can we arrest the decline of the Universalist churches, and turn the tide toward greater successes both of numbers and of churches and greater influences?" (*The Christian Leader*, February 1, 1941, p. 108). But there was no response. Twenty years later the Universalists merged with the Unitarians.

After Universalism celebrated two hundred years as a denomination in 1993, it is time to respond again to the question: What is the remedy? The remedy I propose is to universalize Unitarian Universalism. This remedy means bringing to bear upon the whole movement a renewal of the Universalist heritage, faith, and mission. The platform of reform for carrying out this remedy is modest, beginning with a few major areas.

The Reform Platform

The *Pia Desideria*, Phillip Jacob Spener's Pietistic handbook for the reform of the Lutheran Church, includes a simple, three-part division: the shortcomings of the church in Spener's time; the possibilities for reform, and practical steps for a renewal of the faith. This division seems relevant to Unitarian Universalism today, although there are great differences in history and theology between the two movements.

Unitarian Universalism at present lacks spiritual

depth and passion—or roots and wings. This malady comes when increasing numbers of newcomers are asking for both depth and passion. While there are many hopeful signs of renewal in the movement, there remains a marginal quality about what kind of spiritual community we might become. What does it affirm? What common values do its members share? How pluralistic is its diversity and what cannot be tolerated in a movement expressing toleration? How can its religious communities acknowledge their Christian roots, while recognizing that the communities themselves are no longer Christian? These are the perplexing and troublesome questions being raised by many Unitarian Universalists. The words of historian David B. Robinson are on target:

> [We are aware of a] feeling or a hunger for a deeper inner life and a more profound experience of the world than we share. We're haunted by the specter of our own superficiality, the uneasy feeling that life is sliding by and leaving no deep mark upon us. . . . We've found ways of dealing with this hunger, or masking it, but we've found it has a curious persistence (*1992 Selected Essays*, UUMA 1992, p. 150).

The Unitarian Universalist movement is passing through a major time of transition, from a movement dominated by the Enlightenment faith in human reason and science to an emerging spirituality—one that has much in common with the Pietist tradition, but is also concerned with building community. The emerging spirituality will remain pluralistic but with much clearer parameters. In fact, the clearer the parameters, the more specific the theology, the stronger the movement will become.

The irony of our hunger is that one source of its fulfillment has been close at hand in the heritage of Universalism, more specifically, in Pietistic Universalism. The needs of depth and passion can be addressed in light of our heritage. In Universalism, the often-vague notion of spirituality is made concrete, specific, historical. The gift of Universalism is that it provides two hundred years of an American spiritual heritage. The central Pietistic need for a deeply personal, almost passionate experience of transcendence is another important wisdom that comes from our past.

In *Return to the Spring,* Unitarian Universalist minister and writer Jacob Trapp sums up the situation:

> There are new stirrings among us these days, away from the Unitarian Universalist parochialism, away from the secular club idea of a church, toward a deeper and more sympathetic understanding. . . . There has been, and there is, a famine in our churches. Well, blessed are they that

> hunger. Blessed are the unsatisfied Unitarian Universalists who hunger for being. . . . The utmost wonder and power and mystery of reality are always around us and within us, but it is we ourselves who are not always there . . . (Trapp 1987, p. 12).

SHORTCOMINGS OF THE UNIVERSALIST FAITH

The *Handbook for Congregational Studies* describes four key dimensions of a congregation:

Program: the organizational structures, plans, and activities through which a congregation expresses its missions and ministry;

Process: the underlying flow of life in the congregation; how it makes decisions; its morale and climate;

Identity: the persistent set of values, beliefs, patterns, symbols, and stories that make a congregation distinct;

Context: the setting, local and global, in which a congregation finds itself and to which it responds (Carroll, Dudley, and McKinney 1986, p. 21).

These four dimensions are applicable to an entire religious movement. I apply them here in terms of

Universalism's relationship to the movement as a whole. Although the denomination calls itself Unitarian Universalist, by and large the Universalist identity has been submerged, hidden, neglected—at least until 1993 when it became important to talk about its two-hundredth anniversary. Until recently, most books about Universalism had been written decades ago. The Universalist Historical Society had been eliminated and few knew anything about the status of the Universalist churches that had become part of the wider movement in the merger. Even as late as 1990, the two-hundredth anniversary of the Philadelphia Convention of Universalists (when articles of faith and a plan for church government were adopted), barely a whisper could be heard. To many, Universalism was a vague relic from the past, little understood, seldom mentioned, and sometimes talked about as a more Christian, less intellectual religion of small towns and blue-collar cities.

The underlying *process* among Unitarian Universalists with Universalist leanings also has been unclear. Morale among the Universalists remaining since the merger has been generally low; state conventions of Universalists, which were once the heart of the governance structure, still exist, but one hardly knows of their existence. Universalist publications are minimal (except for the Universalist *Herald*, the longest continuing publication in the denomination). Traditional Universalist conference centers, such as Murray

Grove, have threatened to close. The more than 1,000 congregations listed in the 1990 Unitarian Universalist Association Directory included only 125 historic Universalist churches (Universalist before the merger), with a combined adult membership of slightly more than 25,000—a far cry from the nineteenth century, when Universalists claimed nearly 700,000 members (the true figure was probably closer to 500,000). In fact, what was called a merger in 1961 resembled consolidation in 1991, with only a small remnant of individuals and churches who maintained strong ties to Universalism.

Few *programs* are in place to renew the presence of Universalism in our movement. State conventions have been weakened; by 1992 in Pennsylvania, for example, the number of Universalist churches had dwindled from fifty to eight churches, only three with memberships of nearly 100 members. Many congregations seem unaware of Universalism's heritage. Sometimes old-time Unitarian churches do a better job of keeping the Universalist tradition alive.

Last, in terms of *context*, morale is low among Universalists: denominational neglect seems real, with smaller historic Universalist churches struggling, state conventions greatly weakened, and a pervasive sense of gloom among those Universalists still gathering. The situation, both locally and globally, could not be much more discouraging.

Possibilities for Reform

There are three basic alternatives for the renewal of Universalism: do nothing, seek to form a separate Universalist organization outside the Unitarian Universalist structure, as either a new entity or part of another denomination, or seek to universalize Unitarian Universalism, which means to reform the Unitarian Universalist Association and its constituent parts so that they more deeply reflect Universalist heritage, theology, and practice.

The first alternative, not doing anything, maintains the status quo. One could expect the present cycle to continue: bursts of energy about Universalism for special anniversaries, followed by long periods of neglect. Facing a similar period of decline, the Unitarians concluded in a 1937 report, *Unitarians Face a New Age,* that if nothing were done "it would . . . be better to liquidate the present organizations and resources, for the mere continuation of any institution after it has ceased to meet a real need is wasteful, and for this to happen to an institution calling itself 'liberal' would be a tragic irony of fate" (American Unitarian Association 1937, p. 3). The same conclusion could be applied to Universalism.

The second alternative, to form an entity outside the Unitarian Universalist Association or to merge with a different denomination, is supported by some Universalists. They believe the 1961 merger was a mistake, and that Universalists would be much better off as a separate movement or as part of another denomination (initially, the Universalists considered merger with the Congregationalists). This is a modern version of the Separatist Pietist appeal for separation from the orthodox establishment to form communities that more closely represented what they considered the New Testament model. The difficulty with such a view is what we have seen in our past—separations may take place, but they often lack the resources to last. However romantically attractive may be the notion of separation, the consequences would do much to harm Universalism when it is weakest. As one learns in working with new congregations, starting a new church as a spin-off in a conflict or at a weakened time in the life of a larger congregation simply does not work.

The third alternative, seeking to universalize Unitarian Universalism, at first seems the most cautious—seeking the path of least resistance, the slow process of reformation. Actually, it may be the most radical, in terms of getting to the root. In fact, our movement is called Unitarian *Universalist.* To ask that the denomination bearing this name actually live up to its name may cause a reformation. It would be similar to a Christian standing up on a Sunday and asking what that particular congregation was doing to be disciples of Jesus. Imagine what might happen in Unitarian Universalism if Universalism were incorporated into the life of the movement.

The best hope for the renewal of Universalism is to *universalize Unitarian Universalism*, to help the movement incorporate Universalist heritage, theology, liturgy, stories, and ethics. Such a process needs to be carefully considered, perhaps as part of a new study of the spiritual needs of the movement. A president of the denomination could make this study a major priority, perhaps advocating for a new Commission on Appraisal report on the emerging spiritual needs and resources of Unitarian Universalism, with a focus on what Universalism has to offer.

I would like to make a few suggestions for reform, based on the Pietistic reforms of the past and my experience as a Unitarian Universalist minister. Just as the Unitarian Commission on Appraisal report in 1937, *Unitarians Face a New Age,* has been one of the most insightful and catalyzing documents of the movement, a new report might serve the same purpose. It might be called "*Unitarian Universalists Face a New Age,*" and describe the emerging spiritual climate, the spiritual resources of Unitarian Universalism, and recommendations for the future.

But to what major issue should reform be directed? The major weakness of Unitarian Universalism at present is that it lacks a clear spiritual focus that might lead to genuine religious community. The issue, then, is twofold: (1) What are the spiritual needs of our present membership and what can we say about the emerging spiritual needs of the next generation? (2) What spiritual resources does Unitarian Universalism bring to bear to meet these needs, or what resources does it need to develop?

Spiritual focus and commitment to community are critical to the future of Unitarian Universalism. How, out of such a pluralistic faith, can genuine community arise? And what specifically is spiritual?

To both needs—spiritual focus and commitment to community—Universalism, especially its Pietist version—has much to offer. In fact, based on the old heritage, I would argue for a new paradigm, a new metaphor other than "individual freedom of belief": Universalist in theology, as well as Unitarian; interdependent in polity and not just congregational; Unitarian Universalist in allegiance to a way of life and not just to a set of principles.

This paradigm alone would set in motion reforms. It would require that the Universalist heritage be understood and a theology articulated. It would mean different forms of governance, ones that seek balance among the various parts of the denominational network. And it would require commitment to a common cause.

Thus far, I have applied the outline of Spener's *Pia Desideria* to Unitarian Universalism: describing the condition of the movement, outlining the possibilities for reform, and finally suggesting a practical series of steps to universalize Unitarian Universalism. Spener offered six basic reforms for the church of his time and some of the themes still are relevant for our religious tradition. Specifically, the creation of small study groups, the doctrine of the priesthood of all believers, the primacy of spiritual life over doctrine, the need for repentance rather than disputes, and the education of ministers all have meaning today.

But Spener's six reforms are directed toward a specific situation among a particular people and for the purpose of reforming the Christian church of his time and persuasion. Reforms are needed today to renew the spiritual depths of Unitarian Universalism by restoring the Universalist presence. I have developed a simple model of how this reform might be conceived, based on the four dimensions of a religious community: identity, programs, process, and context. In each case, I have made a few basic recommendations. (See chart at the end of this chapter.)

Pietism has been criticized for its inward, sometimes other-worldly emphasis, its stress on individualism rather than social application, its sometimes overly optimistic view of human nature, and its underestimation of the categories of sin and judgment.

Pietism has been seen as a threat to prevailing orthodoxies. In the case of Unitarian Universalism, the prevailing orthodoxy was a post-traditional Enlightenment faith. Pietism struck hard at this tradition with its excessive rationality and individualism. Pietism represented a political threat to the prevailing order. What kind of order might religious authorities maintain if Pietists could read and interpret the Bible for themselves, meet without clergy, and have religious experiences normally mediated by clerics? The priesthood of all believers is a much-lauded doctrine as long as no one tries to live it.

Paul D. Kuenning's *The Rise and Fall of American Lutheran Pietism,* offers many parallels to Unitarian Universalism:

> One result of the defeat of American Lutheran Pietism was predictable, for losers rarely fare well in the eyes of history. Pietism has remained one of the most misunderstood and maligned movements within the church of the reformation, especially in North America. It became the whipping boy, upon which Lutheran theologians and historians . . . heaped uninhibited diatribes. . . . It was occasionally paid the compliment of having contributed a warmth of feeling, depth of devotion, and charitable concern to the Lutheran heritage. . . (Kuenning 1988, p. 2).

Unlike the Lutherans, Unitarian Universalists have acted with more indifference and neglect than hostility toward Pietism. An unreflective, passive disinterestedness has reigned, a long history of denial. Yet in Kuenning's conclusions about why Pietism is important to Lutherans, the same five, rewritten for Unitarian Universalists, are appropriate:

1. A renewal of the positive elements of the Pietist legacy could immeasurably enrich the diversity of Unitarian Universalist theology and life.
2. Pietism could provide us with a deeper understanding of Protestant Evangelicalism today, which is the fastest growing segment of the Christian church and perhaps connect us to this movement on various issues of common concern—world hunger, war and peace, etc.
3. Pietism's insights could help us clarify the theological base for social justice into living faith instead of simply talking about it.
4. Pietism could help our movement reconnect with other movements, such as the Society of Friends, Mennonites, Brethren, Schwenkfelders, Methodists, and Lutherans.
5. Pietism offers us a renewal of the old Universalist sense of hope.

This last proposition contains the most powerful reason that Pietism is essential to the future of Universalism. For those who struggle with God's grace and human evil, with a generation nurtured on skepticism about the future of the human enterprise and the planet itself, a new understanding of hope is difficult to swallow. The old Universalist notion of a loving God who will not finally let us go may still have meaning. It is the story of a creation that is worth saving because we are loved, of a spirit that calls us to repentance and renewal, and of our responsibilities to each other and this planet as stewards of Life. It is a Universalist call to recognize in each other the children of a common parent, huddled together in risky times, but bound together nonetheless by what Spener called "common creation" and "common love."

The words of George Huntston Williams in *American Universalism* ring true:

> The formative Universalist confidence [is] that there is a powerful and benign force at work within us, about us, at the interior of our being and above it, which sustains our hope. . . . We can . . . count on more than "good luck" for the century ahead, not wholly because of the inherent and unambiguous goodness of men—on this we have been sobered and perhaps even alarmed—but because of the sustaining powers of the cosmos, which, as Universalists so early perceived, is at once our celestial and our earthly home. . . .

> May all these forbearers . . . help us . . . to reach "the mother nature in the most refractory" and to perceive the divine paternity in all men, and all this because we have reglimpsed the vision of John Murray, as he once in England knelt and prayed directly to "dear planet earth," deeply sensible . . . of the Almighty, the ultimate *mysterium et fascinosum*, whose awesome compassion will not let a single soul or atom get beyond his purposeful love . . . (Williams 1976, p. 89).

A Platform for Reform

To universalize Unitarian Universalism is to be Universalist in theology, interdependent in polity, and Unitarian Universalist in allegiance. To do this, there must be structural changes, attitudinal/behavioral changes, and a renewed world mission in our denomination.

Identity

Goal: To reestablish the Universalist identity (values, beliefs, stories, symbols) within Unitarian Universalism.

Means

1. Nurture research and publications about the origins of Universalism, particularly its early Pietist roots.
2. Require ministerial candidates to become familiar with Pietistic Universalism.

3. Provide religious education materials for adults and children on early Universalism, including resources for church school and home study. These materials should include the stories, personalities, music, and liturgies of Universalism.
4. Develop a new journal of theology and history with a focus on Universalism.
5. Begin a denomination-wide series of small, focus groups to study the early history of Universalism to articulate what Universalism means to participants.

Process

Goal: To improve the morale of Universalists within the larger movement and create a means for their inclusion in decision making.

Means

1. Establish a commission on appraisal to study the present and future spiritual needs of Unitarian Universalists, especially younger adults.
2. Establish a network of small study groups (conventicles) as part of the process above, to explore the issue of spirituality, particularly Universalism.
3. Explore how best to develop alternative forms of spiritual community (i.e., retreat centers) to continue the networking process.

Programs

Goal: To renew the Universalist presence within the movement.

Means

1. Ensure that ministerial students receive training in Universalism.
2. Explore the creation of a Lay Ministry Center to provide training to lay people as "missionaries" to act within their congregations and districts as teachers of Universalism.
3. Establish an affiliated Universalist organization within the denomination to plan, coordinate, organize, and evaluate all programs related to these reforms.
4. Create an ad hoc group of religious leaders to articulate and disseminate a Universalist theology, doctrine of the church, public theology, and plan for diversification of the movement.

Context

Goal: To form an international association of individuals and organizations to extend Universalism worldwide.

Means

1. Create and build an international association of people and organizations whose mission is to extend Universalism.

2. Sponsor conferences and workshops on issues related to a global theology and interreligious cooperation.
3. Publish and disseminate the proceedings of such conferences.

APPENDICES

These include "The Pietist Tree" and "Starting Spiritual Growth Groups in Unitarian Universalist Congregations," a basic primer.

If you are using this book for a discussion group on the Pietist tradition, the Tree can be used as a handout. Two additional readings should be assigned: *Pietists: Selected Writings,* edited by Peter C. Erb (New York, NY: Paulist Press, 1983) and "Pietism: A Much Maligned Movement Re-Examined" from the magazine, *Christian History* (Vol. V, No. 2, available from *Christian History,* Box 540, Worcester, PA 19404, $3.00).

The Pietist Tree: Links Between Europe and America

Proto Pietism, or "German Spiritualism"

The sixteenth-century roots of Pietism: Anabaptism, Spiritualism, and Evangelical Rationalism. Its leaders included Casper Schwenkfeld (1490–1562), Jacob Boehme (1575–1624), and Johann Arndt (1555–1621).

George Huntston Williams claims that Pietism can be seen as a grandchild of the radical reformation, especially its Anabaptist roots, and that a line of influence exists between Schwenkfeld, Boehme, and Arndt and Phillip Jacob Spener, the "parent" of Pietism. Among the earliest of the Universalists in America, Dr. George de Benneville, Schwenkfeld, and Boehme were well known; indeed, de Benneville was doctor to many Schwenkfelders in the Oley Valley, Pennsylvania.

The Rise of Pietism in Europe

Seventeenth-century European roots were established by Phillip Jacob Spener (1635–1705). The publication of Spener's *Pia Desideria* in 1675 marked the official beginning of Pietism.

Pia Desideria is considered the springboard for the Pietist movement. Spener's tendencies were to reform from within; he hoped to continue Luther's reformation, not supplant it, by stressing the study of the Bible, the priesthood of all believers, and a more practical training of pastors. Though Pietism took many forms, for matters of simplicity here are two major developments:

Churchly Pietism

Classical German Pietism sought to reform the Lutheran Church.

August Hermann Franke (1663–1727) was its chief leader after Spener, initiating many practical reforms. The University of Halle, Germany, was a Pietist school, from which came many of the first missionaries to America.

Radical Pietism

Separatist Pietism sought to form new groups closer to the New Testament. Gottfried Arnold (1666–1714) was its earliest leader. Out of this movement grew a great deal of activity, from the Moravians to the Brethren, and others.

The Rise of Pietism in America

The effect of European Pietism on religious life in early America was deep, rich, and diverse. From the Churchly Pietism reforms of Spener and Franke came Henry Melchoir Muhlenberg (1711–1787), a guiding leader in Lutheranism. From the Separatist/Radical Pietists came a host of Pietistically oriented movements in America. From Count Zinzendorf (1700–1760) came the Moravians; Johan Conrad Beissel (1620–1768) founded the Ephrata Cloisters; from Johann Kelpius (1673–1708) came a religious community in Philadelphia; from Ernst Christian Hochman von Hohendel (1670–1721) came the Brethren. Moreover, other groups such as the Society of Friends, German Baptist Brethren, Dunkards, Shakers, Methodists, and Universalists were influenced by the Pietists.

George de Benneville (1703–1793), considered the first preacher of Universalism in America, had direct contacts with the radical or sectarian Pietists in Germany before coming to America. In America, he helped Christopher Sauer publish the first German-language edition of the Bible. He lived among the followers of Schwenkfeld and was a frequent visitor to the Ephrata Cloisters. His mid-eighteenth century homestead in Oley, Pennsylvania, was based on a Pietistic house church model. According to Charlotte Irwin, a scholar of Pietism and Universalism, de Benneville is the link between radical, separatist Pietism and early American Universalism. In 1726, 100 German Pietists came to the Oley Valley, about twenty years before de Benneville.

The three earliest and greatest originators of Universalism in America were raised in Pietist environments or had early contact with such environments: John

Murray with Pietistic Methodism in England; Elhanan Winchester with the Baptists, and Universalism's great early theologian, Hosea Ballou, also with the Baptists.

The earliest expressions of Pietism in American Universalism were confined more to the colony of Pennsylvania, with its large German population, than elsewhere. Pennsylvania was a haven for many religious groups, in contrast to Massachusetts, which was controlled by one religious group. Many of the early German Pietists settled in Pennsylvania. Close to here, in New Jersey, John Murray preached a Universalist sermon in a chapel built by Thomas Potter, a Friend and Universalist. It was in Pennsylvania that George de Benneville settled and Elhanan Winchester later started a Universalist church.

But even New England offers traces of the influence of Pietism on Universalism, in the hill country of New Hampshire, Vermont, Western Massachusetts, and Maine. In these areas, a radical/evangelical/Pietistic Universalism emerged, which can be seen in the ministries of such persons as Caleb Rich (born 1750).

Starting Spiritual growth Groups in Unitarian Universalist Congregations

Spiritual renewal is not a quick fix or easy process. It can be painful, usually takes time, and must include people in decision making. Often its results cannot be seen for decades. Every reformation begins with one small step.

A reformation from the top down may work faster, but never commands commitment. Lasting reformation occurs person to person, cell to cell, congregation to congregation, congregation to world. Therefore, the larger vision that sets the background for this outline is nothing less than the reformation of Unitarian Universalism to make it fulfill its own mission of being an inclusive, spiritually grounded world faith. Such a mission requires that we begin somewhere; in a tradition based on congregational polity, there is nowhere better to begin than with people.

Growing by Subtraction, Not Addition

Congregations grow by subtraction, not addition. We are conditioned to think of church growth as adding members to an existing body; but, in fact, the more small cells or groups there are within a church meeting specific needs, the more likelihood there is for overall growth. In an often anonymous and impersonal world, many people yearn for the closeness of an extended family. One of the greatest vehicles for growth among Unitarian Universalists in this century was the fellowship movement, a network of lay-led, loosely organized groups arising in the 1960s and 1970s. While most of these groups did not last, they fulfilled a need for small, caring cells, spaces where people could know each other by name.

Taking a cue from the fellowship movement, the insights of the human sciences about small groups, and my experiences in the parish, I reflected on how this principle of growth by subtraction—multiple small cells within a single congregation—might be applied to Unitarian Universalists.

Models for Spiritual Growth Groups

Various paradigms exist for meeting the three dynamics of a spiritual growth group: personal growth, interpersonal growth, and intrapersonal growth.

The personal growth model involves becoming aware of one's own spiritual needs and developing a means to meet them. Growth occurs when needs and goals are understood and met through responsible behavior in relation to self and significant others.

To experience this model, I took a workshop at Princeton Theological Seminary led by Roy Pneuman. The learning theory used was a laboratory theory, in which people first experience something. The following diagram illustrates the theory at the heart of the process (from *The Learning Process* by Margaret Bruehl and Roy Pneuman):

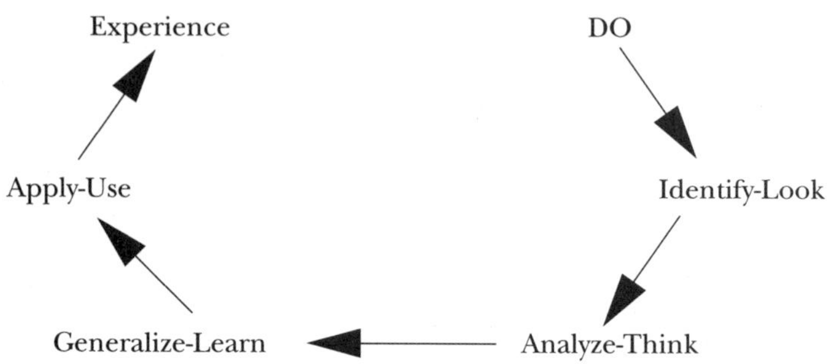

The days usually began with opening meditations, silence, visualizations, yoga, or other methods of relaxation. Using the model above, the experience of doing something set the tone for the rest of the day—whether taking a test (Myers-Briggs, for example) or constructing a banner. After the experience, group members would help each other reflect. Eventually the whole group would reach some understandings. Finally, each person would take this understanding and apply it to his or her own life. The intent of the process was more than personal renewal; it was to experience, not just think about experiencing, community.

The *interpersonal model* for spiritual growth involves ourselves in relationships to others, the connections we make or fail to make (including our relationship to

God). The interpersonal model assumes that we cannot be spiritual by ourselves, but stand in relationship to others, including those we love as well as those with whom we have difficulties.

I explored this model in the work of religious educator Thomas Groome. His primary concern is how people come together as a religious community. He sees a six-fold process:

1. Focus (A story with an issue is presented.)
2. Own Our Action (People are invited to respond.)
3. Critical Reflection (People are asked to reflect.)
4. Community Story (What does the tradition say?)
5. Dialogue (How do we feel about our tradition?)
6. Vision (Where do we go from here?)

This was the basic model I used to start a spiritual growth group in a local congregation (see the next section on The First Day Group, a spiritual growth group affiliated with the Unitarian Universalist Congregation of the Wyoming Valley, Pennsylvania).

The *intrapersonal growth model* involves the idea that our spirituality should be related to the world in which we live and those with whom we do not have regular contact. Especially we should seek to live out the faith we proclaimed.

Two written resources are valuable. One is a book, *Social Analysis*, by Joe Holland and Peter Henriot, which presents a model for relating faith and issues of social justice. A second valuable resource is *A Manual for Starting an Action/Reflection Group in Your Church* by Arvid Straube, a minister in Durham, North Carolina. He has been working with the issues of liberation theology and how they might apply to a predominantly white North American denomination. His groups also begin with action, not reflection.

The First Day Group—Basic Guidelines

1. These guidelines may be changed as needed, by consensus of the group.
2. We are a spiritual growth group, not a therapy or discussion group.
3. We will begin by meeting once a month as close to the first day of the month as possible for no more than two hours, beginning promptly at 7:00 p.m. The group, by consensus, may agree to change this schedule.
4. This is not a casual, drop-in group. We are committed to meeting at least once a month. Except for illnesses, emergencies, or being out of town, your presence is expected.

5. Our sessions are confidential. Whatever we talk about, unless decided otherwise by the group, remains in the group.
6. We are all leaders. We will take turns leading groups, being the focus person, copying materials, etc.
7. This group will not accept any new members past (determine a date).
8. We will be honest and loving with each other, practice active listening and letting each other speak.
9. The basic process for each of our gatherings will be:

   - Opening Worship (silence, spoken thoughts/prayers)
   - Check-Ins (Each person is given the opportunity to share whatever she/he wants.)
   - Focus Person (One person, a month ahead, is named a focus person; this means he or she has one half hour of uninterrupted listening to do whatever he/she wishes: a spiritual or life journey, discuss a life or spiritual issue, etc. The focus person may ask for help, feedback, or guidance, but only when asked may the group respond.)
   - Open Discussion of Readings (The group itself decides on what to read as a group. The person bringing a shared reading must also provide copies for people to read.)

- Praxis (The group reflects on how the congregation itself can grow in spiritual depth.)
- Business (Any business items discussed. Consensus rules, which means that even if one person is not in agreement no decision can be reached.)
- Check-Outs (Each person is given a chance to give a brief idea of what is ahead in the month.)
- Closing Worship (Five minutes of silence or spoken words as people decide.)

The primary preliminary purpose of the group was to hear each other's stories, essentially the major part of Thomas Groome's model of how a religious community comes together. I selected this process to help a group start for a number of reasons:

1. We usually do not take time to hear each other or our life journeys and this process gave people a chance to tell about themselves.
2. Our religious communities tend to be diverse; hence, it is important that we learn to listen to each other (in one group, for example, six were raised in the Catholic tradition, two in the Presbyterian, and only one as a Unitarian Universalist).
3. To hear each other's stories in a supportive environment is the means for beginning to

learn to trust each other.

4. Storytelling is a spiritual exercise, and stories are the stuff out of which theology can be formed.
5. Hearing each other's stories takes time, and it took eight months, but the process was necessary for anything else to follow.
6. While some attention was paid to personal renewal, this was not a primary purpose initially; nor was intrapersonal growth a goal, because people first needed a sense of group identity.
7. Utilizing Groome's process, I intended to have personal stories relate to our UU tradition.

In starting your own group, be as clear as possible about its mission.

1. The group should reflect on the three dimensions of spiritual growth—personal, interpersonal, and intrapersonal—to consider what it needs and desires. The old rule "form follows function" is true here; the purpose of the group will shape its activities. Consider adopting a holistic approach to spiritual growth, taking into consideration the personal, interpersonal, and intrapersonal dynamics.
2. Early in the meetings, the group should be introduced to the history of Unitarian Univer-

salist spirituality, with special attention paid to the early Universalist Pietists, such as Dr. George de Benneville.

3. Use the laboratory theory of learning as a model, since it begins from experience and responds more readily to the real-life situations of participants. This model can easily be adapted to fit any group. For example, simply having people telling their spiritual autobiography is beginning with their experiences; the group then helps that person identify issues, analyze them, learn from them, and apply any lessons learned.

The group should be structured to meet personal, interpersonal, and intrapersonal spiritual needs over a sufficiently long enough period of time to permit the process to unfold. Preliminary commitments from group members need to be made to cover something of the following kind of covenant:

I commit myself to:

1. Meeting with our group every two weeks for one year, only missing meetings because of special emergencies.
2. Spending at least ten minutes a day in private meditation, prayer, silence, or other spiritual practices and to keeping a journal based on

such practices.

3. Considering with the group how we might express our spirituality in the world.
4. Keeping the meetings of the group confidential.
5. Listening to others.
6. Helping out in various leadership roles in the group to share responsibilities; roles might include conducting worship, providing refreshments, keeping the group on time and on track, etc.
7. Reading whatever materials the group determines important for its own development.
8. Checking in with the group before I make a decision to leave it.

Once the initial composition of a group is set, it should not be altered if possible. The group process takes time to build trust; adding one new person can change completely the nature of the dynamics, as can one person dropping out.

At the beginning of the group process, a gatekeeper should be appointed, perhaps in rotating role. The gatekeeper is the person who keeps the group on track, makes sure everyone has a chance, pays attention to the process, gives feedback, and keeps the group within reasonable time constraints. Rotating the gatekeeper role will give everyone a chance to learn.

Every group will test out the process that best meets its needs and this process should be reviewed and changed as needed. Some crucial parts of the regular meeting are:

- Opening Worship
- Check-Ins (A time for each person to take a few moments to bring others up to date on her or his life.)
- Storytelling (Perhaps giving a half hour to one person per meeting to talk about himself or herself, any life issue, spiritual issue, etc.)
- Tradition (Could be shared reading and discussion of the Unitarian Universalist heritage.)
- Community Focus (On a specific issue of the local, national, or international community, with brainstorming on something the group can do, particularly personal, direct action, such as the group participating in a Habitat for Humanity project or going to a soup kitchen, etc.)
- Congregational Focus (A monthly reflection on how the small group is helping the larger group, the congregation.)
- Closing Worship (Perhaps, in the Society of Friends style, this might be gathered silence and brief "spoken ministries." Prayers for each other in the group might be appropriate).

The group process might begin more smoothly if the spiritual growth group begins with a weekend retreat, to help the group coalesce more easily. The following is an outline for a weekend retreat, although each group will need to find its own retreat style and content.

Spiritual Growth Weekend Retreat

The purpose of the retreat is to give people a sense of what the group is like, to get to know one another, and to share religious journeys.

Friday Night

1. Dinner together.
2. Introduce the laboratory method of learning.
3. Talk about covenant or commitments for group (hand out list of commitments).
4. Paired introductions (people pair off, get to know one another, and come back to introduce other person to group).
5. Closing vespers (brief).

Saturday Morning

1. Breathing, relaxation exercises, silence.
2. Check-ins (How are things going?).
3. Talk about commitments list. Clear up confusion, get consensus.

4. Spiritual reflections (a time for people to talk about what each one means by spirituality and what they need from a group). Have participants write down some thoughts after the discussion.
5. Present the three dynamics of spirituality and indicate that the group will seek to work in all three areas.
6. Create a banner (see instructions at the end of this section).

Lunch

Saturday Afternoon

7. Share banners. (In groups of three to four, each person is given time to share banner; the other people in the group are invited to name what they see.
8. Groups reconvene. (Let each group share what they discovered. Suggest that each person put a banner on the wall. Suggest that over a break, people walk around and look at the banners.)
9. Break.
10. Presentation of Unitarian Universalism, the basics, with a focus on Universalist Pietism. Discussion.
11. Sharing our religious pasts. In one large group, go around the circle three times. Let people answer each question in turn, with no discussion: Round 1: In what religious tradition, if any, were

you raised?

Round 2: What parts of that tradition have you left behind? (If no religious tradition, someone might focus on family tradition.)

Round 3: What parts of that tradition have you saved because they are worthwhile?

Dinner

Saturday Evening

12. Open discussion and sharing. What spiritual disciplines, if any, are people now practicing? Keep a running list. When completed, ask group to talk about which ones they feel are crucial to the spiritual growth group.
13. Closing vespers.

Sunday Morning

14. Opening worship.
15. Check-ins.
16. Creating a group banner. Go around again to look at individual banners. Ask people to work together on one banner to represent this group. Give no instructions as to how to do so or what to do. It's up to the group.
17. When banner is completed, ask the group to explain what it means.
18. Closing business. Set future meetings of group, select any initial leaders, discuss readings, details

of the group such as time, place, days, etc.

19. Check-outs. Close by asking people to reflect on this time together and their hopes for the group.

Lunch and departures

To Create a Banner

Excerpted from "Role Functions in a Group" by University Associates.

Draw your banner outline on newsprint and, following the key, use a word, short phrase, or symbol to describe yourself in the areas listed below. You may refer to the impressions you wrote down following the reflection period.

Key

1, 2, 3, 4: Create four symbols (pictures) that represent your deepest, most cherished values. Do these in order of importance (1, 2, 3, 4). Use written statements (short phrases or words) to describe the following:

5. Who am I?
6. My happiest moment or experience or greatest achievement.
7. Three things I do well.
8. Three areas, traits, characteristics, or attitudes I want to improve.
9. Personal motto by which I (try to) live.
10. One thing I would like to have said about me if I died today.

11. Three things I would *like* to learn to do well.
12. Three accomplishments I want to realize during my lifetime.
13. Three things I would like to start doing now.
14. My three highest priority life goals.

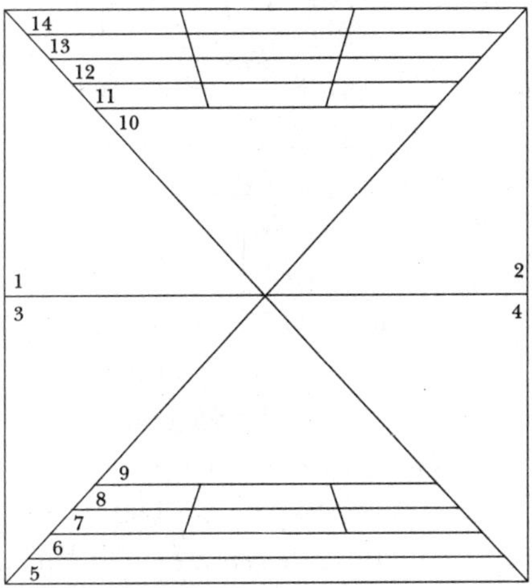

Bibliographic Note

This bibliographic comment reflects the major divisions of this work: Pietist roots in Europe and America; the fall of American Pietistic Universalism; growth, decline, and spiritual ferment among Unitarian Universalists, 1961–1992; and universalizing Unitarian Universalism.

Introductory but comprehensive resources for exploring the rise of Pietism in Europe are: Dale Brown, *Understanding Pietism* (Grand Rapids, MI: William B. Eerdmans, 1978), an easy-to-read summary of Pietism's history, themes, and major figures. A companion piece is Peter C. Erb (editor), *The Pietists: Selected Writings* (New York: Paulist Press, 1983), which contains an excellent introductory section, plus the writings of early Pietists, such as August Hermann Francke, Gottfried Arnold, and Count Zinzendorf. Two books by F. Ernest Stoeffler are especially important: *German Pietism During the Eighteenth Century* (Leiden, Holland: E.J. Brill, 1973) and *Continental Pietism and Early American Christianity* (Grand Rapids, MI: William B. Eerdsman, 1976). To understand "Proto Pietism," a book by George Huntston Williams is enlightening, *The Radical Reformation* (Philadelphia: Westminster Press, 1962). An understanding of Pietism from a Lutheran perspective is Paul D. Kuenning's *The Rise and Fall of American Lutheran Pietism* (Macon, GA: Mercer University Press, 1988); of special interest here is Chapter 1, "German Roots."

A good, basic text of Jacob Phillip Spener's *Pia Desideria* has been edited by Theodore G. Tappert (Philadelphia: Fortress Press, 1967) with an excellent introductory chapter. A more popular, easily read introduction to Spener and his classic book is Marie E. Richard's *Phillip Jacob Spener and His Work* (Philadelphia: Lutheran Publication Society, 1897). A more scholarly, detailed summary of Spener, focusing on his life and the times around the time of the publication of the *Pia Desideria* is Allen C. Deeter's *An Historical and Theological Introduction to Phillip Jacob Spener's Pia Desideria: A Study in Early German Pietism* (Princeton, NJ: Princeton University, doctoral dissertation, 1963).

Probably the best, most comprehensive treatment of the rise of Pietism and Universalism in America is an unpublished master's thesis by Charlotte Irwin, *Pietist Origins of American Universalism* (Boston: Tufts University, 1966). Sydney Ahlstrom's *A Religious History of the American People* (New Haven: Yale University Press, 1975) has an excellent chapter, "The German Sects and the Rise of Pietism," a general overview of Pietism's effect on many early American religious traditions. Only one book provides a more complete description of the "parent" of American Pietist Universalism: Albert D. Bell's *The Life and Times of Dr. George de Benneville* (Boston: The Universalist Church of America, 1953).

Two books by Clinton Lee Scott have limited materials on Pietistic Universalism. One, *These Live Tomor-*

row (Boston: Skinner House, 1987), has a chapter on the life of George de Benneville; a second, *The Universalist Church of America* (Boston: Universalist Historical Society, 1957) has a chapter on Pietistic Universalism in Pennsylvania. In this book, Scott makes the intriguing assertion that the future spirituality of Unitarian Universalists might have to do with the religion of de Benneville.

General books about Universalism are helpful for background; among these are: John Coleman Adams, *Universalism and the Universalist Church* (Boston: Universalist Publishing House, 1915); Ernest Cassara, *Universalism in America* (Boston: Skinner House, 1984), a documentary history with source materials; Russell E. Miller, *The Larger Hope: The First Century of the Universalist Church in America, 1770–1870*, probably the most detailed account of the rise of Universalism, but limited in terms of Pietist Universalism; Elmo Arnold Robinson, *American Universalism* (New York: Exposition Press, 1970), broad but not very enlightening; David B. Robinson, *The Unitarians and the Universalists* (Westport, CT: Greenwood Press, 1985), with excellent, well-written chapters on Universalist history and theology; Ernest F. Stoeffler, *Continental Pietism and Early American Christianity* (Grand Rapids, MI: William B. Eerdmans, 1976), while not specifically detailing Universalism, is a classic text on the rise of Pietism in America; Stephen A. Marini, *Radical Sects of Revolutionary New England* (Cambridge, MA:

Harvard University Press, 1982), a remarkable history of the rise of three radical sects in New England: Free-will Baptists, Shakers, and Universalists; L. B. Fisher, *A Brief History of the Universalist Church* (Boston: Young Peoples Christian Union, 1904), a simple introduction to the denomination; M. Hale Smith, *Textbook of Universalism* (Salem, MA: John P. Jewett & Co., 1845), another general introduction; George Huntston Williams, *American Universalism* (Boston: Beacon Press, 1976), an analysis of the various strains of Universalist theology around 1870; an interesting review of the decline of Universalism is in an article by R. S. Kellerman, "The Decline of the Denominations" (Boston: *The Christian Leader*, February 1, 1941).

A few books and articles relate directly to Dr. George de Benneville. Principal among them are: Albert D. Bell's *The Life and Times of Dr. George de Benneville* (Boston: The Universalist Church of America, 1953); Elhanan Winchester, *Some Remarkable Passages in the Life of George de Benneville* (Germantown, PA: Converse Cleaves, 1890) was published without de Benneville's knowledge or approval; various sermons, notes, and medical entries by de Benneville also may be seen in their original form in the Schwenkfelder Library, Pennsburg, Pennsylvania, and in the library of the University of Pennsylvania; a descendent of de Benneville has also written a brief biography, George de Benneville, *Dr. George de Benneville* (Boston: Universalist Historical Society, May 26, 1931); Cynthia Edson's article, "A History of Universalism in the City of Reading" (Reading, PA: Historical Review of Berks County, 1975) summarizes de Benneville's life in the Oley Valley by the then-minister of the Universalist church in Reading; another general overview of de Benneville is Elmer Schultz Gerhart's "The First Preacher of Universalism in America" (Reading, PA: Historical Review of Berks County, October, 1948); Peter G. Bertolet's "Fragments of the Past, Historical Sketches of Oley and Vicinity" (Oley, PA: Women's Club of Oley Valley, 1980), is a brief biography of de Benneville; de Benneville's place in the radical reform movement can be reviewed in David A. Johnson's "George de Benneville and the Heritage of the Radical Reformation" (Boston: *Universalist Historical Society Journal,* 1969); a wider treatment of the radical reformation can be found in George Huntston Williams's, *Spiritual and Anabaptist Writers* (Philadelphia: Westminster Press, 1962).

Other related works on the origins of Universalism include: Paul Siegvolck's *The Everlasting Gospel* (Germantown, PA: printed by Christopher Sauer, 1753), considered the text read by most early Universalists, certainly by de Benneville; Stephen L. Longnecker, *The Christopher Sauers* (Elgin, IL: The Brethren Press, 1981), the life of the man who took de Benneville into his home and with whom de Benneville worked on printing projects; and E. Digney Baltzell, *Puritan Boston and*

Quaker Philadelphia (Boston: Beacon Press, 1979), for a general overview of the religious climate in colonial Pennsylvania as contrasted to Boston.

Finally, to understand the changing nature of Universalist covenants consult *The Articles of Faith and Plan of Church Government, 1790* (Philadelphia: Joseph P. Justice, 1818) for the results of that meeting; *The Universalist Centennial of 1870* (Boston: Universalist Publishing House, 1870), for the proceedings of this gathering and an introductory speech on Universalist theology; *Principles and Purposes of the UUA* (Boston: UUA, 1985), the statement of the denomination, which also has a study guide with all previous covenants.

Other worthwhile books for looking at the changing covenants of Universalism include: Paul Chestnut, *The Universalist Movement in America* (unpublished doctoral dissertation, Duke University, 1973), a general introduction to the changing theology; A.J. Mattil, *The Evolution of American Universalism* (Gordo, AL: Flatwoods Free Press, 1992), contains the words of all Universalist covenants and a review; John C. Morgan and Thomas Chulak, *Mission Covenant* (Boston: UUA, 1987), which argues that covenant is the central organizing metaphor for the movement; John C. Morgan (editor), "The Pennsylvania Universalist," (Reading, PA: Vol. 32, No. 1, October, 1990), a review of Universalism in Pennsylvania and the 1790 Philadelphia Convention; C. Conrad Wright, *Walking Together: Polity and Participation in Uni-*

tarian Universalist Congregations (Boston: UUA, 1986), a classic statement of the central role of covenants in liberal religion.

The best overview of growth and decline among Unitarian Universalists is probably still *Unitarians Face A New Age* (Boston: American Unitarian Association, 1936), a study carried out by the Commission on Appraisal; this publication not only sets out the issues, but lays the groundwork for their solutions and ushered in a period of growth known as the "Unitarian Renaissance." Interesting interpretations of the movement have been made by Peter Spilman Raible, among them: *Fellowships: A Report Card After Twenty Years* (Boston: Unitarian Universalist Association, 1971), a review of the strengths and weaknesses of the movement; *Church School and Church School Decline* (Boston: Unitarian Universalist Association, 1971), a report indicating that the real crisis was in declining church school enrollment; and *Population Trends in the Unitarian Universalist Association* (a report presented to the Commission on Appraisal, December 1978). See also my 1983 study "Growth and Decline Among the Unitarian Universalists," commissioned by the UUA Extension Department (Boston: UUA, 1983).

Other general books on church growth among Unitarian Universalists are: Dorothy T. Spoerl, *A Brief Look at the History of Extension* (Boston: Unitarian Universalist Association, 1978), an overview of growth and decline among Unitarians and Universalists; Lon Ray Call, *A Research On Church Extension and Maintenance Since 1900* (Boston: American Unitarian Association, 1946), a study by one of the founders of modern extension work among Unitarians; James R. Hutchison, *Growth and Decline: Trends and Speculation* (a paper delivered before the Unitarian Universalist Advance Conference, October, 1978), one of the most honest descriptions of the Unitarian Universalist decline; and *Report of the Religious Education Futures Committee* (Boston: UUA Board of Trustees, October 1981), a report describing the emergent pluralism of the movement.

Works of a more statistical or quantitative nature include: Frederick Wiseman, *UU World Readership Survey* (Boston: Unitarian Universalist Association, 1978), an analysis of the attitudes of readers of the denominational magazine. Two publications that describe the fellowship movement among Unitarians—the major growth vehicle in this century—are Laile Bartlett, *Bright Galaxy* (Boston: Beacon Press, 1960) and Monroe Husbands's *7 Life Preservers for Unitarian Universalist Fellowships* (Boston: Unitarian Universalist Association, 1962). Peter Raible's *Fellowships: A Report Card After 20 Years* (previously mentioned) is a more sober evaluation of the demise of fellowships, not just their growth potential.

General books on church growth and decline include: Dean R. Hoge and David A. Roozen, *Understand-*

ing Church Growth and Decline (New York: Pilgrim Press, 1979), an excellent, comprehensive analysis of American church trends; and Russell J. Hale's *Who Are the Unchurched?* (Washington, DC: Glenmary Research Center, 1977).

Three resources for understanding the emerging spirituality among Unitarian Universalists are: Robert B. Tapp, *Religion Among the Unitarian Universalists* (New York: Seminar Press, 1973), which makes the case for a posttraditional religiosity; *The Quality of Religious Life Among Unitarian Universalist Congregations* (Boston: Commission on Appraisal, Unitarian Universalist Association, 1989), an analysis of the religious values and needs of a cross-section of Unitarian Universalists; and *1992 Selected Essays* (Boston: Unitarian Universalist Ministers Association, 1992).

For additional reading on the issue of identity as part of a religious tradition, a general introduction is Jackson W. Carroll, Carl S. Dudley, and William McKinney's, *Handbook for Congregational Studies* (Nashville: Abington Press, 1986), especially Chapter 2, "Identity." A resource on identity in Unitarian Universalist congregations is John C. Morgan and Tom Chulak, *Mission Covenant* (Boston: UUA, 1987).

In assessing the emerging dimensions of a spirituality for Unitarian Universalists, three books by James Luther Adams are comprehensive and thought-provoking: *On Being Human Religiously* (Boston: Beacon Press,

1976), *The Prophethood of All Believers* (Boston: Beacon Press, 1986), and *An Examined Faith* (Boston: Beacon Press, 1991). A small volume of essays by Jacob Trapp, *Return to the Springs* (Boston: Unitarian Universalist Association, 1987) is good, as are meditations by Unitarian Universalist minister Gordon B. McKeeman, *To Meet the Asking Years* (Boston: Unitarian Universalist Association, 1983); a collection by African-American Unitarian Universalists *Been in the Storm So Long* (Boston: Unitarian Universalist Association, 1991) is excellent, as is *Cries of the Spirit: In Celebration of Women's Spirituality*, edited by Marilyn Sewell (Boston: Beacon Press, 1991).

About the Author

John C. Morgan, a Philadelphia native, has been a Unitarian Universalist minister for over ten years, serving local churches, two districts, and the Unitarian Universalist Association. Morgan holds a Master of Divinity degree from Andover Newton Theological School and a Doctorate of Ministry from the Lutheran Theological Seminary of Philadelphia. He is a contributing writer to the *Friends Journal* (Quaker) and associate editor of *The Universalist Herald*, the oldest continuing liberal religious periodical in North America.